INTRODUCTION

PLEASE NOTE.

In the interest and context of his
includes some language and ter
policies and medical terminolog
previously used to describe patients, such as the terms,
'idiot', 'defective', 'insane', and 'imbecile' are rightly no longer
appropriate and can appear insensitive or upsetting. They are
now considered derogatory, abusive, and offensive. I will
endeavour to put these words in 'inverted commas,' to show
that their use is no longer acceptable.

CW01499696

Name changes.

1845-1846: Originally named Shropshire and Wenlock Borough
Lunatic Asylum.

1846-1851: Changed to Shropshire and Montgomeryshire
Counties and Wenlock Borough Lunatic Asylum. Shropshire

and the Welsh county of Montgomery shared the institution to
help manage the cost, having first overcome language
difficulties.

1851-1863: Shropshire and Montgomeryshire and Wenlock
Borough, Shrewsbury and Oswestry Lunatic Asylum.

1864-1911: Lunatic Asylum for the Counties of Salop and
Montgomery, Shropshire and Montgomeryshire and Wenlock
Borough.

1911- 1921: Shropshire and Borough of Wenlock Lunatic
Asylum. After the agreement between Montgomery and
Shropshire ended, 150 patients were moved out of the
hospital.

1921-1948: Salop Mental Hospital. In 1947 it had its highest population, 1000 patients.

1940-1941: The Copthorne and Shelton Emergency Hospital. Temporary title during World War 11.

1948-2012: Shrewsbury Hospital Shelton. Shortened to 'Shelton Hospital' before closing.

1997: The Marches, a brand-new admission unit built on the site. This included Stokesay and Whittington Ward, a new ECT Suite, Pharmacy, the multigym and League of Friends shop.

They joined it on to the Occupational Therapy department.

Shelton remained the main hospital.

2012: The Redwoods Centre, a new £45m 'mental health village,' opened to replace Shelton. The 10-acre site with four buildings contained 116 beds. It was part of a 50-year plan to modernise mental health care provision. The Redwoods is built behind Shelton and is halfway between it and the Royal Shrewsbury Hospital.

Unfortunately, we can't interview the original attendants, doctors and patients. We have to rely on records preserved, diaries found and old medical journals to get a glimpse of what life was like early on. But with our 1.3K members of the 'Shelton Hospital Community 1845-2012' Facebook group, we have lots of information and material about its history and, of course, tales of paranormal sightings passed down.

It wasn't uncommon to have three or more generations of staff working there in both the past and more recent times. I am privileged to have had so many group members and other staff from my organisation, sharing both their parents' and grandparents' stories passed down. Unsurprisingly, though, the majority came from night staff and occurred around 'the witching hour.'

SPIRITS OF

SHELTON

INCLUDING HISTORY
& PAST TREATMENTS

1845-2012

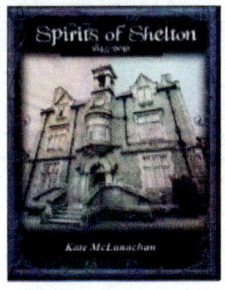

FORMER SHROPSHIRE 'LUNATIC

ASYLUM' AND

PSYCHIATRIC HOSPITAL

Kate McLanachan

Printed in the United Kingdom.
For more information, or to book an event, contact:
Katemclanachan.author@gmail.com
Book & cover design by Author

ISBN: 9798321465936

Second Edition: March 2024

Kate McLanachan

CONTENTS

SPIRITS OF SHELTON

I will endeavour to tell you a few of them from colleagues and our group members who include:

retired staff - nurses - hospital visitors - volunteers - local people - porters - domestics - administrators - secretaries - occupational therapists – physiotherapists – doctors - psychiatrists - student nurses - health care assistants - nursing assistants - enrolled nurses - matrons - social workers - estate technicians - ex-patients - relatives of staff and patients - IT workers - anaesthetists - librarians - patient's bank staff - advocates - gardeners - hairdressers - youth training scheme staff - social care staff - nurse tutors - pharmacists - cooks - chefs - kitchen staff - advocates - managers.

I was one of those staff who trained as a Registered Mental Nurse at Shelton Hospital in 1989, so have a 35-year career at the time of writing for the same organisation. I never once left the service, but moved to community nursing posts, which meant I still visited patients admitted to Shelton Hospital until it closed. I met my husband Pete there when we were student nurses. My adult sons have no intention of following in our footsteps. My great aunt was a psychiatric nurse in Manchester.

Two years after closing, I was fortunate to get briefly involved with Shelton Hospital Heritage group and took photographs of the deserted hospital before they converted it into houses and apartments. We entered the first time as staff who knew the building well but returned with 2 community staff who had never worked there, but who were psychic mediums. I include their experiences, which were both intriguing and unnerving.

The reason for starting the Shelton Facebook group was to prevent the loss of photos and information by sharing them. The members have made it a collection of fascinating memories of times gone by. 'The Redwoods', a modern mental health facility with en-suite bathrooms, replaced one of the last of the old Victorian institutions that is now gone for good. So different from the 'nightingale dormitories.' Light and spacious, unlike Shelton, with its small windows and wards which had a corridor layout symmetrically designed to segregate male and female patients.

"A far cry from the Victorian Shelton Hospital asylum it replaced and an emblem of a 21st century approach to supporting people with mental health issues," Andrew Hughes, Project Director of the Trust said. "A big and revolutionary change, not only for Shropshire, but the whole region."

But what is clear from the comments and posts on the Facebook page is that, while things had to move on, change and improve, many of the people connected to Shelton Hospital miss it greatly. It offered respite and time to heal with a strong community spirit in a self-contained space. I still see patients who say how much they miss Shelton or who have fond memories. But I am aware not everyone who walked through its doors would feel the same. The experiences patients may have had in the days when the hospital was understaffed and overcrowded, and treatment ineffective or barbaric, would have been very different.

CHAPTER 1
THE CHAPEL

"If her walls could talk, they might recount the stories of generations of families, of two World Wars of prayers she has heard, of joys she has shared, and somber times of sorrow, grief, and loss."
— Arlene Stafford-Wilson, Lanark County Comfort—

I was told a fabulous ghostly story by a well-respected, very experienced community nurse named Bonita, who had also previously worked on the wards at Shelton Hospital. She had taken a short career break and attended a 'return to work interview' at Shelton Hospital with two of our managers, Mr Zihni Chelik and Mrs Gill Foster.

Bonita wasn't a hundred percent sure as she left the building whether she would accept the offer of a return to work. At least she knew they would happily take her back, but there were other personal matters to consider. Walking through the beautiful tree-lined grounds, the flower beds bursting with well-tended blooms, memories of her happy times nursing there came flooding back.

She had parked her car by the hospital chapel, built in 1854-6, where there was an expectation that all able patients attended the two Sunday services back in the day. At one service in 1885, they counted 368 patients. Male patients and staff entered through one door sitting on the right, and female patients and staff sat on the left. The chaplains once permanently employed here were long gone.

Occasional services were the norm these days, with a minister coming from the local parish churches. A patient's own clergyman would attend on behalf of a patient if requested.

Bonita stopped briefly on hearing the pipe organ playing inside the chapel, recognising the hymn, 'Great is Thy Faithfulness,' sung by many angelic voices.

Great is Thy faithfulness

Great is Thy faithfulness

Morning by morning, new mercies I see

All I have needed Thy hand hath provided

Great is Thy faithfulness, Lord, unto me

Summer and winter and springtime and harvest Sun,

Moon and stars in their courses above Join

with all nature in manifold witness

To Thy great faithfulness, mercy, and love.

She could see the candelabra torches once used for gas lighting, brightly shining from where she stood, looking up at the side of the chapel. Moving towards the door, she stood listening for a while. The door had a 'green man' figure on both sides that captured her gaze. There were four altogether, on both of the north doors, with varying degrees of leafy foliage sprouting from their stone faces. Symbols of rebirth, representing the four seasons and cycle of growth, renewed each spring. This door had examples of both the 'Foliate and Disgorging heads,' secular figures adopted by Christianity in 19th century Gothic Revival.

Bonita suddenly felt compelled to see the choir of voices stood in lines in their pews in the aisles facing the pulpit. It was a sunny day and the light would be shining through the stained-glass window with its image of St Luke, the patron saint of artists, doctors and surgeons. Dedicated to the hospital's Medical Superintendent, Dr Arthur Strange (1872-1902).

Approaching the door, the scent of burning holy incense wafted through the keyhole. As Bonita's hand touched the handle, the organ paused, the singing stopped mid-sentence, and an eerie silence descended like a cloak. The door had a padlock on it, rendering the chapel presently out of use. Bonita became aware the lights, sounds and smells had disappeared instantaneously. The choir of phantom voices was no more.

Stepping back, she felt a sudden icy chill despite the warm summer's day. She smiled, wide eyed. Any doubt she had experienced now put aside, she drove home and telephoned the manager straight away to accept the job. The whole encounter left a great impression on Bonita. It symbolised the changes in the four seasons and the cycle of life, as in the words of the hymn and the changing faces of the green men.

It somehow represented new beginnings, and the changes required to move on from the past, although recognising it as only ever a flicker away. Dreams of the future are so often tinged by echoes of the past, shown in a captivating tale of hope and personal growth. Bonita had encountered nothing of this nature previously, but will never forget her experience. She returned to nursing for another two decades, contributing her vast experience to her nursing team and those in her care using her skills, knowledge, and compassion for others.

The Chapel

CHAPTER 2
THE BALL

"To those capable of seeing the light of these spiritual orbs, there is no darkness, for they dwell in the presence of limitless light and at midnight see the sun shining under their feet."
— Manly P. Hall—

Sandy, a regular contributor to the Shelton Facebook page, who nursed at the hospital for several years, relayed a strange sighting she experienced when on duty. She described it happening on a night shift, many years ago, on Maple Ward. This was a mixed sex ward for older people with 'functional mental illness', which relates to conditions other than dementia.

Sitting quietly in the day area, with all her patients settled and asleep, she watched through the open door down the dimly lit corridor, observing the area and listening for any movement from the bedrooms, as night staff do. Sometimes patients awoke distressed or in need of help, which was Sandy's job once all were in bed. Her colleague was making them both a hot drink in the kitchen, which was further down another corridor, at right angles to the bedroom passage.

Suddenly, something emerged from one bedroom, but not a person. It was an object. Not that unusual, and she quickly recognised it as a ball. Her first impression was that someone must have thrown it from their bed, as the doors were all left slightly ajar. Or perhaps a patient had just turned over and inadvertently kicked the ball off their bed. It may have been one of those soft squidgy stress balls, but it didn't make a sound. It was a white ball which she could only describe as repeatedly bouncing around from wall to wall, as if it had a life of its own. But she would have expected it to lose energy, as every time a ball drops and moves back up after a bounce, it has less and less kinetic energy. The air slows it down and it cannot reach the same height unless hit with a bat or thrown back with the same force.

The ball was bouncing up and down the walls of the corridor on both sides, missing the bedroom doors and moving at varying heights, but, most strange of all, it moved as an illusory experience of slow motion. It then disappeared. Sandy stared transfixed, unable to move and quite relieved to see her colleague approaching with two steaming mugs of tea. She was not afraid, but on reflection, felt it had to be paranormal. Several years later, it happened again to Sandy on night duty. This time on The Rowans, a ward for younger people with dementia.

There is no real, plausible explanation for this experience of altered perception and 'slow motion' speed of a moving object, other than Akinetopsia. But that is an extremely rare neuropsychological disorder, often described as seeing motion like a cinema reel or a multiple exposure photograph. It is a dysfunction of brain networks responsible for visual perception of speed. Brain fog, tiredness, anxiety and 'the menopause' are all other reasons for this phenomenon, but everything else was at normal speed and Sandy felt fine.

She was not the only person to see this spectacle played out in front of her. It happened to Lorna in a different decade, on the same ward. Lorna, another nurse, had read Sandy's much shorter account on our Facebook page. The striking similarity of her own experience astonished her. She messaged me her full story and agreed I could include it in my book to share with a wider audience. Lorna and Sandy did not know each other. Both nurses were unaware of just how similar their experiences were, as they had shared more details privately. This is from Lorna.

Kate McLanachan

"Hey Kate, I wanted to share my experience of 'the ball' on Maple Ward with you. I was working with a student nurse and it was about 3 a.m. We were sitting in the dining area with my chair facing towards the bedroom corridor. The student nurse was on my left and didn't have the same view. We were having a friendly chat when I looked down the corridor and saw something white appear. My immediate thought was that a patient had thrown something through their bedroom door. I stood up to go down the corridor but stopped in my tracks when I realised it had come through the wall just past the second bedroom on the right. In the room opposite was a dying patient, whom we were checking more regularly.

The ball was white, about the size of a small melon and slightly fluffy, like a big cotton wool ball. It seemed to go into slow motion and take ages to bounce before disappearing into the wall opposite. Now I always thought if I saw anything like this, I would be terrified, but the most incredible feeling came over me as I watched the ball. It's difficult to describe, and some people may laugh, but a feeling of deep, inner peace came over me as I watched the ball, as if someone had touched my soul. Sounds dramatic, I know, but I have never experienced that feeling before or since, and the memory of that feeling has stayed with me over the years. It was so beautiful.

Of course, the poor student nurse thought I'd lost the plot as she saw nothing and kept asking me what was wrong. I couldn't speak to her for ages, as I was so mesmerised. I think I put her off nights for good! I still often wonder what it was? I thought maybe it was 'someone coming' for our poorly patient, but he didn't pass away that night or for quite a while after, so I don't believe it was that. I believe that whatever it was and for whatever reason, it definitely came from the 'other side'. I haven't spoken about this a lot and thought I was the only person who had experienced it, so it sent shivers down my spine when I read Sandy's post."

You might wonder, like me, if they could be 'orbs? People often report seeing them as floating balls of light when seen with the naked eye. Also known as orbs of light, energy orbs, spirit orbs, or ghost orbs, and described as self-illuminating, translucent spheres of various colours, including white. Orbs can be anything from as small as a few centimetres to up to 12 metres in diameter.

When they appear in photographs or in a recorded image, they can appear as white, round glare spots, also known as 'orbs.' This is due to specs of dust particles floating in the air, or on the lens. Or sometimes it's insects, mold spores, or pollen, which are illuminated by the light of the flash when you're taking a picture. When the flash catches these particles just right, the light reflects out of focus and creates the 'ball' of light that we see.

Others believe the 'energy orbs' they see around them, or in their photos, are a spiritual vehicle for a loved one, an angel or guide, to move from one realm to another. Most orbs are pure white and thought by some to be a tiny manifestation of protective energy. Others think they are sent to help us or to bring us a message. Many describe them as 'fuzzy', a bit like Lorna's "fluffy cotton wall ball." Like Lorna, it is common to describe feeling 'mesmerised,' with a sense of safety and no fear.

The only other similar sighting that might explain this is ball lightning, a rare and unexplained phenomenon described as luminescent, spherical objects that vary from pea-sized to several meters in diameter. Though usually associated with thunderstorms, when observed, this phenomenon lasts considerably longer than the split-second flash of a lightning bolt. It's highly unlikely though, as they reportedly leave behind a strong sulphurous smell, explode, and sometimes kill you. There were no storms reported on these nights either.

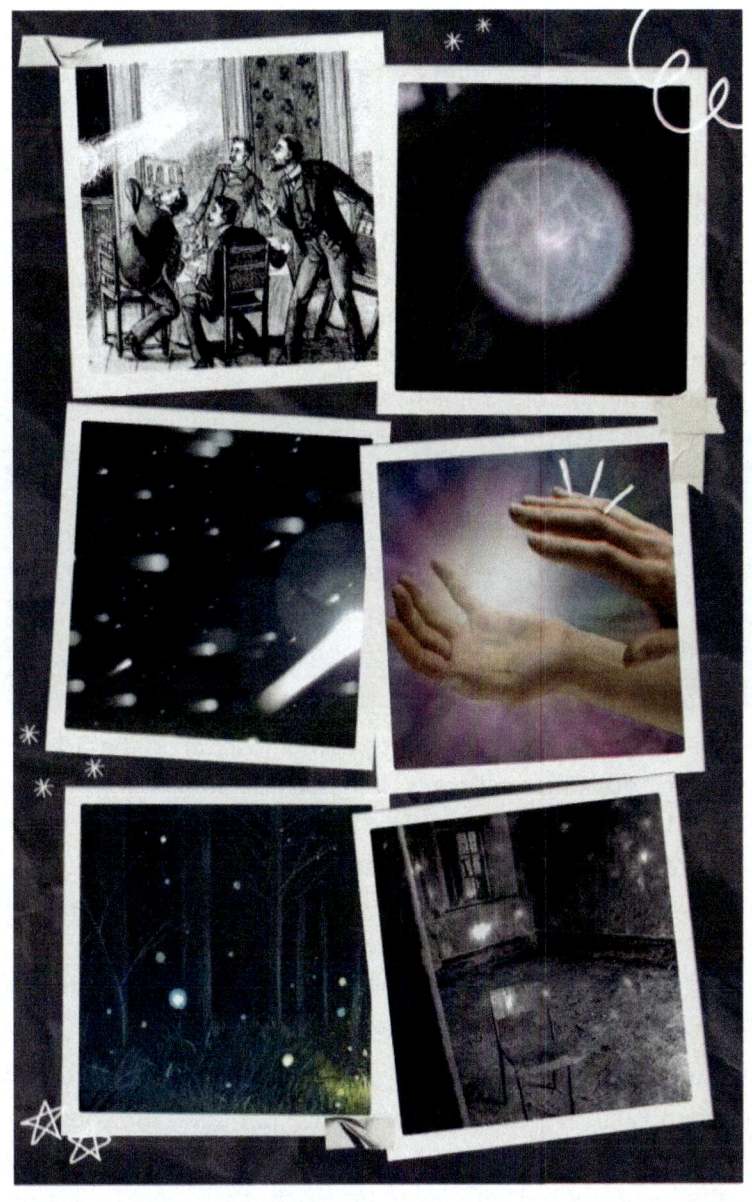

CHAPTER 3

THE SMOKE ROOM

It is important I make my patients unidentifiable for reasons of confidentiality, even if posthumously. It is obviously out of respect, but also a very important statement in my professional code of conduct that I uphold as good practice. The duty of confidentiality continues after a patient has died. Although what happened endeared us to him even more and, knowing him, I don't think he would have minded me using his name, but I won't, so I'll call him Stuart.

This all happened before community mental health teams were fully in operation, with more capacity to respond to everyone who needed it. I'm sure you're thinking it still has a long way to go to meet the population's needs now and I wouldn't disagree, but the NHS, as always, needs more funding.

Housman Ward was at the back of the hospital on the first floor overlooking the Chapel. It admitted patients occasionally, but primarily received transfers from other wards with patients who required 'intensive psychiatric care,' as we referred to it then. They came from acute admission wards, rehabilitation wards, and sometimes elderly wards, and only if the parent ward could not safely manage their needs. It existed before we had 'high dependency areas,' attached to wards.

Stuart had been on our ward for several months, which wasn't that unusual. We even had one of two patients who couldn't be nursed anywhere else and were with us for years. Many patients presented with paranoid psychosis, severe or agitated depression, hypomania, or Korsakoff Syndrome and we had a higher staff-to-patient ratio and a smaller number of patients on the ward. Patients reported feeling "safe" on Housman. We had a locked door, but patients had the freedom to move around without being followed everywhere. It rarely took long for them to settle enough to go out for walks and transfer back to their main ward.

Over the years, staff from different eras described working on Housman Ward as hugely rewarding. You had to learn to be more relaxed and laid back, but approachable and ready to stop any incidents occurring as a team. We strived to provide high-quality, person-centred, specialised care in a smaller ward environment and patients responded well to us.

When I was there, I was one of the four 'Control & Restraint' trainers for the hospital. Seclusion wasn't a thing anymore. We also trained the hospital staff in breakaway techniques. I remember the best course I ever did was the ENB 956 'Managing Violence and Aggression.' It was about deescalating potential incidents, both verbally and non- verbally. The aim was to reduce the need to resort to using any physical restraint by defusing the situation. It was very effective and was always the first option for staff where possible. We also learned how to 'debrief' following any incidents.

We replaced 'C&R' with more effective, fewer hands-on 'MAPA' training, which stood for 'Management of Actual or Potential Aggression.' It then moved to the current 'DMI', which is 'De-escalation Management & Intervention' training. It is a holistic approach that looks at risk assessing and putting care plans in place to allow for the earliest possible nonphysical interventions to take place. Also, it provides staff with the skills to handle situations that may require a physical intervention.

Back to Stuart, he was a quiet, contemplative chap who appeared to never miss a thing happening around him. Although who knows really what is going on in another person's head? Stuart had this self-assured body language that commanded respect from others. He was a big man in his 50s. Some people described him as more 'bad than mad.' This was a concept passed down from decades back, maybe originally over a century ago. It was possibly because he apparently had a criminal record too. There were always some patients admitted who proved to have no mental illness and were trying to prove 'insanity' or 'mental illness,' to get out of something.

We saw Stuart as a socially isolated man, who suffered paranoid delusions and had a personality disorder, but he responded well to a combination of compassionate, respectful care, tailored to his needs alongside medication. Unfortunately, he always stopped taking it upon discharge, leading to relapse, and this often got him into trouble. Stuart spent most of his time on the ward in the smoke room, which was still in use at that time. It was a room off the long dining area corridor, which had the day room at one end and the female dormitory at the other. The toilets were further along, as was the kitchen on the opposite side. The bathrooms were off the dormitories. It was a mixed ward and had several side rooms that used to be padded cells and later seclusion rooms with high barred windows. These rooms were now used for patients with high levels of agitation or, if actively risky, to themselves or others. They contained just a bed and when in use, there was a constant observation from staff.

Some new staff were initially wary of Stuart. He was more unpredictable when admitted, unmedicated and floridly psychotic. Not 'bad,' at all. He was a proper gentleman. I remember a colleague on night duty on Clive Ward getting 'jumped on' by a male patient and Stuart intervening to stop him. When Stuart was ready for discharge, he went straight from our ward to the men's night shelter, as had no fixed abode.

During the 1990s and until 2006, a charity ran the shelter for the homeless. It initially was in the Old School House beside the Welsh Bridge, and later at 70 Castle Foregate. Here there was space for up to 12 residents. Vacancies always filled up immediately. Unfortunately, the government withdrew funding for the 'Supporting People' programme in 2006. With the high costs of providing supervision on the premises every night, there was no option but to close the shelter.

Not long after his reluctant discharge from the hospital, someone informed the staff that Stuart had sadly passed away. Found alone in his room at the shelter. He had succumbed to cardiac arrest. Stuart had sat quietly on the ward but responded well to treatment, especially the company, attention and care by others, so this was tragic to hear.

Stuart's funeral announcement was in the obituary column in the Shropshire Star. My colleague Avril and I read it together. I can clearly remember us opening the paper over the double laundry trolley in the dining area, outside the smoke room and Avril reading it out loud.

Suddenly, the heavy sash window near to us, that took two hands and all your weight to push down, slammed shut. We both looked up. "That was Stuart!" we both said in agreement with a smile. Neither of us were afraid or felt he meant us any harm. Housman Ward was one of the few places in his recent life where he had felt accepted and not judged, and he had never really wanted to leave. He had returned to where he felt safe and well cared for.

Kate McLanachan

THE APPARITION

A colleague sent me this story from when he worked as a night coordinator, a job title replaced with 'nurse manager,' in the late 1980s. I will call him Nigel as he emailed me privately.

Nigel recalled a cold winter's night while doing his rounds, checking on staff and gathering information for the next day. Near the Porter's Lodge, he had his own office and was the 'go-to' person for staff when they needed anything or help with a disturbed patient. He took external calls about urgent admissions during the night and had many other roles, I'm sure. Not a job many of us wanted as very solitary and carried a lot of responsibility.

Years ago, night staff had to stand up when managers entered the ward. Some suffered from 'night nurse paralysis' a condition where you cannot move your muscles or speak because you are falling asleep or waking up, but your brain is active. It can be scary as the person is fully conscious yet aware they cannot move, but it's harmless. Like sleepwalkers, they are best left to come around unless in danger. Unlike sleep walkers, the muscles can become so rigid, it would take considerable force to move the subject aside. This could happen to you when either sitting, standing, walking, alone, or with others. It can last from a few seconds to several minutes. Disrupted sleep patterns, often seen in shift workers, link to it. Shift workers may feel more anxious about falling asleep on duty or continuously tired because of lack of sleep.

Nigel described arriving at Housman Ward between 2 a.m. and 4 a.m. He was on first-name terms with his staff, as they were with him. It was a different era, with no standing to attention, but visits always occurred during the 'witching hours.' These are the hours where 'night nurse paralysis,' and supernatural events like ghostly presences are most commonly seen. The hour also corresponds with the 3 a.m. peak in the amount of melatonin in our bodies.

As he entered the ward, Nigel described looking straight ahead towards the large bay window opposite the office overlooking the cricket field. There he saw a lady sitting in only her nightdress, with her eyes fixed, staring towards the field. In appearance, she was tall with long, grey hair and barefooted. He went into the office where two staff, a male and a female, were busy doing some paperwork.

On inquiring why one of the female patients was up sitting only in her nightdress on such a chilly night, they rushed out as had heard no one get up. They returned almost immediately, saying, "There is nobody there, Nigel. Only Sue (another nurse, name changed), by the TV lounge, who has closed her eyes and put her feet up as it's her break."

Indeed, when he went back out to look, there was no lady sat in the chair by the bay window. The only strange thing was that Sue was now sitting bolt upright, looking towards the window as if in some sort of trance. Nigel beckoned to the other nurses who came out hurriedly, thinking the woman in the nightdress had reappeared. Sue was coming round, but looked a little confused. "Night nurse paralysis," said the male nurse. "I've seen it twice before."

Nigel asked Sue what she was staring at, but she couldn't say. She hadn't seen the woman as Nigel had hoped, but felt very uneasy and sensed something by the window. Just to be sure, the female staff nurse had gone to check on the female patients and found no evidence that any of them were awake or had been up. None fitted the description of having long, grey hair, either. All the male patients were fast asleep, too. Mentioning this encounter later on to some older staff on his round, Nigel was told that it must have been "the grey lady," whom other staff had also reported seeing, but rarely on Housman Ward.

So, I asked group members on our Shelton Hospital Facebook page, who else has seen the grey lady?

CHAPTER 5

THE GREY LADY

"My gaze followed his. Did I see an outline of palpitant gray like a mist that the sun is about to pierce, wavering, luminous? Did I catch a glimpse of a face with deep-set eyes, more agonized and pitiful than any human face I ever saw?"

— Cornelia A.P. Comer, "The Little Gray Ghost" (1912) —

Dr O'Keefe, an associate professor at Buckinghamshire New University said that the fact that nurses on night shift are awake at the 'darkest, coldest time of the night', known as the witching hour or the devil's hour, may be significant to what they experience.

"I think it's 4 o'clock in the morning specifically, which is meant to be the time when you're most likely to see a ghost, the time when your brain is most tired."

During his career, Dr O'Keeffe has investigated countless supposed ghosts and hauntings and said, "No matter what ghost story I hear, there is always the potential for a rational explanation. But it would be arrogant of me to say, 'That's what happened.' You can hypothesise about natural explanations – either psychological or environmental – but that's all you're doing. You're hypothesising."

Shelton Hospital had an apparition, a woman veiled in grey, unable to find her final resting place. Her pale figure is reported to appear around 3 a.m. gliding along the same ward, only to disappear as she turns towards the bathroom area. Grey ladies, as the name implies, are the grey-coloured ghosts of women. Their faded, transparent image gives them their neutral or achromatic colour, so they are 'without colour'

Some people consider these spectres to be the spirits of women who are believed to have died prematurely without fulfilling their purpose. They also often repeat actions over and over again, like a recording. A chill in the air often accompanies them, along with a sense of overwhelming sadness. Silently treading the halls, dormitories and corridors that once were their home.

The ward that was originally called 'Laundry ward' (before my time), became 'Willow Ward,' then the 'Crisis Team' had 10 short-term in-patient beds there, before it became 'Haughmond ward,' for patients with learning disabilities. I believe Shropshire Homes now has converted this area into Leighton Park apartments and named it 'Esio Lodge,' providing supported living accommodation for clients with autism. It is the ward with the most paranormal sightings.

Willow was a long stay dementia ward, known as an EMI ward which stood for 'Elderly Mentally Ill.' Val is now a retired nurse, but will never forget her first stint of night duty as a 19year-old student on Willow ward. She was briefly sat on her own observing the length of the bedroom corridor, when her eyes captured a movement ahead. It was a women's ward, and she could just make out a lady in a white gown moving up the dormitory before turning towards the toilets. At that time,

only one patient could mobilise independently, but she was slow and stiff on walking. This lady seemed to glide with ease down the passage and disappeared from view as she turned right. It took some time before Val built up the courage to check on the dormitory, after the woman did not return. She found the toilets to be unoccupied and the only patient it could have been was fast asleep in bed. Val added that despite working 10 years on nights, she is still afraid of the dark!

Another sighting of the 'grey lady' as she became known, came from retired nursing assistant Pat, who was working night shifts on Willow Ward. Several hours had passed, and the ladies were settled and asleep. Again, it was that quiet period in the very early hours of the morning when most of the living were sleeping, around 3:30 a.m. Pat saw someone walking across the ward as if they were going to the toilet. Surprised, she went to see who it was, but there was no one in there. She checked all the beds and found the patients were all sound asleep. The room appeared to be freezing just for a few minutes. The lady she saw had long grey hair and wore what looked like a flowing, off-white nightdress, which was why she thought it was a patient. She had nothing on her feet. Others Pat had worked with on Willow had seen her too.

Adrian, who describes himself as a non-believer, saw a 'grey person,' on the ward clearly one night. It was when the ward was Haughmond. A patient spoke about seeing this apparition often at night and said it didn't scare him at all.

Ydna worked nights on the ward when it had beds allocated to the Crisis Team. When alone on duty, he found it very spooky, and every night at 3:00 a.m. he noticed the lights would flicker and doors automatically shut. He found it very unnerving and always sensed there was someone or something at the other end of the ward. Strangely enough, he said he never went down there alone to investigate!

Larry was sometimes on night's covering breaks on Haughmond ward. He described an odd feeling, watching the dormitory from the lounge area at night. A domestic who previously cleaned Haughmond ward between 2001-2009 detected an "eerie presence" in the bottom dormitory and didn't like to stay there alone for too long.

KateMcLanachan

Grey
LADIES

CHAPTER6

WANDERING SOULS

"Last night I saw upon the stair, a little man who wasn't there. He wasn't there again today. Oh, how I wish he'd go away…"
—William Hughes Mearns, "Antagonism"—

Chestnut Ward had a high level of paranormal activity reported by several staff. Jackie (name changed), described one night shift where they had a male patient who was near the end of his life and was expected to pass away peacefully in his sleep. Jackie checked on him frequently, and during the 'witching hour', found him lying flat on the floor beside his bed. Shocked and horrified, she called her colleague Janette (name changed) and they quickly attended to him, but could not work out how this could have happened? He would have had to have crawled over the cot sides to get out and fallen hard on the ground, but there was not a mark on him or a sound made, and his breathing and observations were normal. It was also felt that he did not have the strength to do such a thing. The patient was lying sound asleep on the floor, undisturbed by whatever had led to him landing there.

Stokesay was a female Acute Admission Ward, built in 1997 as part of a new unit. It also housed Whittington Ward, its male counterpart. The building called 'The Marches' connected to the Occupational Therapy Department, built in 1982. Patients nursed there were from Shrewsbury and the West of Shropshire. Sharon, a nursing assistant on Stokesay Ward, told me her ghost story, which was even more poignant as I had known the patient well. Anna, as I will call her, had frequent long admissions to Shelton, with extreme highs and devastating lows because of her illness, manic depression now called bipolar disorder. Often, she would remain uncommunicative or preoccupied with whatever troubled her mind. Over recent years, she had probably spent more time in the hospital than out.

Although she was not on the ward when Sharon was last on duty, it did not surprise her to see Anna on her return from her two-week holiday. As she walked through the dining area to the nurses' office to attend the night handover, she saw Anna sat in her nightdress on a table with her legs swinging. She remembers saying hello to her as she walked past. Anna didn't reply and appeared to be looking ahead at nothing in particular. The only slightly strange thing was that she was sitting on the table rather than a chair.

After the last patient was 'handed over,' with reports on all needs and requirements and day staff passed the keys to the night nurse in charge, Sharon asked, "Have you forgotten Anna?" If it wasn't for their sad expressions, she would not have believed what they told her. As it was, she still walked across to the glass window to look out and check, but could see only the space that Anna's ghost had filled. Sadly, she had made several attempts on her life in the past and unbeknown to Sharon, Anna had committed suicide when Sharon was on annual leave.

Sharon was told Anna had sadly passed away in Intensive Care at the Royal Shrewsbury Hospital, following her suicide attempt. Anna had survived a previous attempt on her life after jumping from an external first-floor iron fire escape on the main building. These fire escapes had concrete steps with metal sides and tops known to some of us as 'suicide cages,' as they reduced the risk of jumping off the top ledge. It did not prevent you from throwing yourself from the top stair to the very bottom, though. Eventually, they added wooden sides and plastic windows and always kept them locked, except in the case of an emergency.

Clare once reported a strange sighting on Stokesay Ward when she responded to the alarm one night. Nurses carried a pinpoint attached to their key chain to be pulled to summon immediate help. They emitted an emergency signal and were used if you needed help to de-escalate a difficult situation. Upon hearing an alarm, Clare ran across from Whittington Ward toward the ward next door. On arrival, she was told there was a very distressed lady in the dormitory area. The nurse in charge handed her the drug keys and medicine card and instructed her to go to the clinical room to draw up an injection.

The staff locked away tablets and injectable drugs in a secure room down another corridor. Here, Clare quickly prepared the agreed medication for the injection. Whilst down there, getting it drawn up to be checked, she heard the second nurse coming down the corridor, so picked up the kidney dish and drug card in each hand. Turning around, she glimpsed the back of someone walking straight past the door. Clare said it literally took 5 seconds to reach the door to call them back, but looking left and right, there was nothing to see. Nobody was there! Seconds later she saw the Duty Nurse Manager coming to check the medication with her, as was protocol when all the other staff were with the patients. She tried to convince

herself that she must have imagined it, but knew she had definitely seen and heard the footsteps of an apparition that day.

Even though Stokesay was a new unit, there was a lot of paranormal activity reported. You will hear soon another story on how spirits 'travel,' so maybe some came from the main hospital to follow the staff they knew on The Marches?

Shelton itself was still open, but the new unit housed the two wards, OT department, Recreation room, ECT Suite, League of Friends shop and the Pharmacy.

Carla knew there was definitely something "amiss" on the ward. One night shift in December around 4 a.m., having just completed a check, she got up to answer the door to the office after hearing a faint knock. A lady stood outside, with cropped light brown hair and fully dressed in a pink turtle or polo neck jumper. On opening the door, though, the figure had disappeared. Carla spun around to check the CCTV on the corridor, the bay and smoke room, but there was no one there.

Another time on Stokesay, Carla saw the back of a lady wearing bright green, walking into the High Dependency Area. Knowing they had a very disturbed lady there; she rushed out to stop her from walking in and waking her. But by the time Carla left the nurses' station and turned the corner, she had gone. Carrying on down the corridor, assuming she must be walking fast, she arrived at the door of the poorly lady who had a member of staff sat outside, but with no sign of the person she had seen. The patient was alone in her room, apparently asleep and facing the wall. Whispering to her colleague, who had seen and heard nothing, the patient suddenly turned over in bed, looked at Carla laughing and said, "She won't talk to you because you're a leprechaun, as you have green eyes. Get out Jezebel." Carla walked away feeling a little disturbed in more ways than one!

Tim reported a very spooky and mysterious tale of a patient he nursed many years ago, who would have more of a connection to him than he could ever have known. I'll change her name to Bertha, even though she is long deceased. When Tim qualified as a staff nurse in 1982, he worked on Chestnut Ward. Bertha was an elderly lady who wore a knitted shawl over her head. In the latter stages of her life, barely able to do anything for herself, Tim remembers often looking after her. She eventually sadly died, which Tim said he guessed was a happy release from her confusion and dementia. Organic mental disorder destroys the mind and, when your body stops working too, life can be just an existence with few pleasures.

As time went on, Tim moved wards and in 1998 bought a bigger house, when his first daughter was born. As she got older, she would wake up with nightmares, calling out to her parents. Rushing to her room one night, Tim found that, once calmed, she described seeing an old lady wearing a shawl over her head sitting at the end of her bed. Tim tried to convince her this was just a bad dream, but it sounded very familiar to him. He searched for the deeds of the house and found that the same 'Bertha' from Chestnut Ward had once owned this house with her husband. This was strange, but retelling the story years later to our Shelton Facebook group, he shared these wise words. "So, to any of you thinking of moving into the newly converted apartments and houses at the old Shelton site, don't worry, ghosts travel."

It is no surprise that as a very old psychiatric hospital, originally a 'pauper lunatic asylum,' Shelton has potentially housed many spirits over its long span of 167 years. So much has changed over that time and structural changes have altered how we see the wandering spirits. John reported the change in floor level, which was raised when Haughmond opened as a refurbished, renamed ward, previously Willow and before that Laundry Ward. The 'grey lady' reappeared, but seemed to have to no legs once they made alterations. Those who still saw her gliding down from the lower dorm to the bathroom knew her as the "half lady." They say ghosts walk in the space they originally inhabited; the new layout is immaterial to them.

Extensions to the hospital led to doors being moved or added. New staircases and corridors that changed the layout over time.

Joe told me about his experience, again, on night duty, which occurred on Wroxeter Ward, our low secure unit. This was formally 'The Rowans', a mixed sex ward for patients with organic illness. Before that, it was Rodney, a male geriatric ward where around forty patients had lived for most of their lives. Looking up from his chair one night, Joe's eye caught a moving shadow in front of him. He stared in disbelief as a male ghost walked straight through the wall of the TV lounge. Now, without looking at plans, we can't determine if there was ever a door there, but they made a lot of alterations on this ward following its change of use.

A week later, Joe recognised the 'ghost' he saw, when standing near the Porter's Lodge waiting for a colleague. The man he had seen was looking towards the camera in a framed picture of the Workhouse on the wall by the patient's bank. Dressed in his old-fashioned clothes, the uniform of a pauper inmate, so similar to that worn at Shelton. Now Shelton was never a Workhouse, but many patients transferred from 'Kingsland House of Industry' and 'Cross Houses Workhouse' in Shrewsbury, plus others, when the purpose-built 'Lunatic Asylum' opened. When they originally built the ward in 1856, they named it Male 17, which it remained for the next 100 plus years. Could this have been the era that this man lived there, with his spirit still walking the corridors as it was at that time?

Catherine remembers working on Rodney and nursing the only patient she ever saw there who had congenital syphilis. Sadly, his untreated mother transmitted it to him at birth. She heard the sucking noise he made with his mouth, as he paced the day room twice in the weeks after he died.

Another nurse, Marianne, was watching a patient on constant observation on Haughmond Ward, sitting outside their bedroom door as they slept. She saw the handle on the door opposite move and it then slowly swung open. It was a vacant room with the door firmly shut and no one else was around. Thankfully, the patient was asleep, as she couldn't move fast enough from that door. Her colleague quickly swapped with her and was unperturbed, but Marianne felt unsettled for the rest of the night and wouldn't swap back.

KateMcLanachan

How 'Haunted Abandoned Asylums'
Are Perceived.

CHAPTER 7

THE GREAT FIRE

TO ALL OF THE PATIENTS WHO LOST THEIR LIVES THAT NIGHT, R.I.P.

Just after midnight on 26th February 1968, a catastrophic fire broke out on Beech Ward. It quickly gained hold on the top floor of the female ward. Sadly, 21 women perished in the blaze and 3 more died later in the hospital. 11 more women suffered serious burns, and many experienced shock and later suffered from trauma. The victims, overcome by toxic fumes, died because of asphyxia and carbon monoxide poisoning. The fire made national news, as it had the highest hospital death toll in Britain in over 14 years.

Beech Ward was home to 43 female patients, and at the time was a long stay ward. The policy of locking patients on their ward was an acceptable practice, although the 1959 Mental Health Act stated this should happen to as "few patients as possible." Back then, staff carried the large skeleton keys marked 'Male' or 'Female,' replaced later when there was less segregation of the sexes by 'Master' and 'Half Master' skeleton keys. Only around 1980, during the decade I underwent training, did the shift to the Yale Key, known as the 'No.1 key, take place.

Most women slept along the 300-foot-long gallery on the window wall, their beds placed 'top to tail. 'The most disturbed patients slept opposite, in side-rooms on mattresses on the floor for their own safety. Patients at the time were mainly elderly and some bed-ridden, but all severely mentally ill.

Staffing levels were low by today's standards, with two qualified nurses and a student nurse to care for 99 patients. Beech staff also looked after Chestnut Ward below, so there would have been one nurse on each ward with the third person alternating to help turn or toilet patients. There were reportedly 800 patients in Shelton Hospital altogether at his time.

Open fires heated wards with fire guards in place. Fire regulations printed as early as 1917 stated that "clothes are not to be dried in front of the fire or on the fire guards," so this was not a consideration by fire investigators. Instead, they determined that a discarded cigarette end, left on the side of an armchair in the dayroom, had caused the fire. The ground floor was undamaged and the 56 patients sleeping there were unharmed. Evacuation took place of 140 patients from the surrounding area, included Chestnut, Lime and Larch Wards.

Rescuers took the survivors to the main hall and served them cups of tea. Please see the photo from the article in the Shropshire Star on February 28, 2018. "50 years on: Deadly Shrewsbury hospital fire which changed thinking forever."

They lay bodies out in the linen room below Cedar Millington Ward, on a row of baths covered with wooden boards which were originally used for hydrotherapy. The mortuary only had room for a few of the deceased.

All reports of what happened that night are very similar, but I have first-hand accounts from staff who worked there with tales of their own experiences. The late Mr Les Mills was a nurse tutor when I knew him in 1989, but he worked at Shelton as a nurse for decades before and lived in the houses in front of the hospital known as 'Shelton Circle.'

Les Mills attended Beech Ward to help evacuate patients. His later account of the fire was that just after midnight, when all the patients were asleep, a nurse smelt something burning. This was not unusual, as gardeners burned green waste just outside Chestnut Ward below but not at night. The nurse apparently investigated, going down the stairs to Chestnut, where she asked the student nurse to go up and take charge of Beech Ward while she had a look around. After finding nothing, she walked through to the far end of Chestnut Ward and up the steps to Beech. On arrival, she opened the door to discover a serious fire and she could not get on to the ward. She fled back downstairs to Chestnut below.

Meanwhile, the student who had been putting an elderly lady back to bed on Chestnut Ward attempted to go up the stairs to Beech Ward, but a wall of smoke blocked her way. Neither nurse nor student could access the ward. They activated the fire alarm and waited for a short time, but could not hear the siren, so pressed the button again. This was a terrible mistake, as pressing it again switched off the fire siren. Staff from around the surrounding area, upon hearing the alarm stop, would assume that it was a false alarm.

The enquiry later confirmed improper usage of the modern fire alarm system. There was apparently a delay of 10 minutes between first noticing smoke and raising the alarm and calling the fire brigade. Two of the hospital's own firefighters attempting to tackle the blaze that night until the fire brigade arrived. They used the hose-cart kept in the garages which connected to fire hydrants, intended only to put out minor fires.

Many local off-duty hospital staff got to the scene quickly. Shropshire Chief Fire Officer Arthur Bloomfeld praised hospital staff for responding "extremely well," to the emergency.

According to him, they rushed to the wing and calmly and orderly led or carried patients out, with no panic. He stated the means of escape at the hospital were adequate. He concluded, "One has to remember that one was dealing with people severely mentally affected and these people cannot be expected to respond in the normal way."

Nicola, a colleague from Shelton, only found out years later how much her dad contributed to the evacuation. Roger Ellis, a charge nurse, was staying with her mum Angie in the nurse's home that night. She was told by the brother of the night porter, who called the fire brigade, that her dad put a wet towel over his head and went back several times to the ward, saving four patients. Apparently, there was a report in the local paper trying to find out who this hero was. Several staff members received medals for bravery, and Dennis Lewis was among them. He returned six times to carry patients to safety.

Seventy fire fighters in twelve fire engines attended the scene to tackle the inferno. Some reports say the fire burned right through to Monday afternoon, but by 2 a.m. it was under better control. A fleet of ambulances took patients to the Royal Salop Infirmary and Copthorne Hospital.

One fire fighter, Mike Bickford, who was there on the night of the fire, had attended false alarms at Shelton hospital previously. As they drove in through the entrance, the fire crew assumed it was just another callout because of a patient setting off an alarm. On arrival at the front of the building, a nurse came running towards them. She climbed up and shouted, "Round the back! Round the back!"

Faced with severe fire and smoke, Mike said, "the cries of the women patients have haunted me since." Fire fighters donned breathing equipment and Nick Morris and George Fletcher were the first inside. They soon brought casualties out, but there were no ambulances yet.

Mike set up an emergency reception area on an empty ground floor ward, pushing beds back. He grabbed a resuscitator called the 'Stephenson Minuteman,' and began moving around those rescued patients to see who was still alive, attempting to save as many as possible. More help was arriving fast. Ambulances were taking patients to the hospital, and the fire had stopped spreading. Fellow officer Jim Prince found a letter saying, "I'm fed up with this effing place," while Mike was sitting down and having a cup of tea. It continued, "I'm going to effing burn it down," or words to that effect. Mike said he thinks they handed it to the Police but does not recall it being used as evidence.

The investigation blamed overcrowding as one cause of the high death toll. Also, beds placed so closely together along the gallery next to the windows made it difficult to evacuate the patients. Many people succumbed to smoke inhalation from the deadly toxic fumes and dense suffocating smoke. The patients on mattresses on the floor survived because they were behind heavy wooden doors which acted as a fire barrier, plus...smoke rises.

Night nurse Kathleen Griffiths, who was in charge of Beech Ward, was accountable for mistakes made with not activating the alarm earlier. However, she was not responsible for the failure found in the hospital of not training night staff in fire procedures and with no instruction on how to evacuate the wards in over 20 years. Also, there was the existence of orders to get the night porter to first obtain the authority of one of the hospital fire officers before calling the fire service.

Matron Rosemary Butters confirmed to the press that they thought the cause was a smoldering cigarette end dropped in an armchair in the dayroom. Her report stated it that was the only locked ward where the most disturbed patients were, and partly the reason for the high death toll. She told the Shropshire Star, "It couldn't have happened in a worse ward than it did. These people are treated as human beings and, as such, they are allowed to smoke. You cannot stop them having a cigarette when they want one and enjoy one. You cannot make them give it up. Some are careless with their cigarette ends. This is a risk which goes with their freedom and privileges."

A member of our group who worked for the fire service had access to the original fire investigation report that looked into the cause of the fire. She shared that the patient who was last to leave the dayroom, and suspected of dropping the cigarette end, had survived the fire.

There was evidence that some patients may have scratched at the windows before either being rescued or overcome with smoke. According to the granddaughter of the Police Officer who did the early plans for the courts, there were blood smears mixed with soot and smoke stains on those window panes that were not broken. My colleague Lisa's mum worked at the time for the secretary and nursing Officer Arthur Morris.

She had the awful job of cleaning sooty blooded rings and other jewellery removed from the deceased and sending them on to bereaved relatives.

The young fire officer, Mike Bickford, told the Shropshire Star that when he visited wards to attend to small fires, the patients would be "standing with their heads bowed, drugged, and in similar clothing. They would be like zombies." The subsequent review of fire safety procedures at hospitals in the Midlands, following the enquiry, brought in changes to fire safety and improved training for staff. Regular fire drills began and training in evacuation and the use of pumps and fire hydrants.

Prior to the fire, 13 years earlier, a public enquiry into conditions at Shelton in 1955 painted a grim picture. Shrewsbury MP Sir John Holt described having the "shock of his life," when he visited. Conditions also horrified Lewis Motley, chairperson of Shrewsbury hospital committee who wanted the building knocked down, describing it as a "snake pit." They criticised the age of the building, "constructed 14 years before the Indian Mutiny," as parts of Shelton, were over 100 years old.

People compared the 1948 film "The Snake Pit" to Shelton and other asylums across the country during that time. I discuss this in more detail in Chapter 11. Thankfully, the attention brought about changes to Shelton. Beech Ward had a nine-month refit and reopened as a rehabilitation ward or 'bridge,' to assist patients in learning the skills to get back into the community. The new look ward had its own dining room, kitchen facilities, reading room, television room, six single rooms and two four-bed dormitories. It accommodated 14 patients of both sexes, as opposed to the original 43.

Treatments on the ward following the refit included Insulin Shock Therapy, Deep Sleep Therapy, Aversion Therapy, and Electroconvulsive Therapy. I will go into more detail about these later on and in my 2nd novel set in Shelton Hospital.

In my time on Beech Ward from the late 1980s, there was Token Economy, a behaviour modification, which rewarded patients who completed daily living tasks or exhibited good behaviours targeted by staff. They could exchange the tokens awarded for privileges or desired items like cigarettes, snacks, recreational materials and hygiene products.

As for the souls of the lost victims, we hope they passed on peacefully. But it was a ward with many paranormal experiences reported by staff.

Decades later, Larry smelt smoke on the fire escape between Chestnut and Beech and, after investigating and finding nothing there, he always felt uneasy and went the long way around. Darren once saw smoke filling the stairwell between the two wards, but there was nothing after he turned away to seek help and then glanced back up. He ran on to the ward, thinking he was responding to a fire, but there wasn't one when he got to Beech.

Shropshire Homes, who renovated Beech Ward 2 years after it closed, discovered burnt beams when they ripped down walls and ceilings. They found a lot of the beams that were blackened still had a strong smell to them. They had to chop some of the beam out, but they boarded the rest over. A Surveyor said he found it very eerie when walking around the ward with boarded-up windows with just a head torch. A builder got spooked because he made the mistake of reading about the fire the day before he went in. Staff often reported the overpowering smell of charred wood when they opened the built-in cupboard in the corner of Chestnuts dining room.

Night staff have experienced some strange, unexplainable occurrences over the decades since the fire. One night, Phil, a qualified nurse, was working with Doris, a nursing assistant, when he noticed she had stopped reading and was looking up and back down with a confused expression. Seeing nothing unusual, Phil asked her what was the matter. Doris replied she had seen burning debris falling from the ceiling and sparks landing on the floor. It all stopped and disappeared quickly, and it left them wondering if it was the anniversary of the fire.

Another night, Phil was on night duty on Beech and sat at the end of the dormitory while his colleague Sarah went for her break at 1a.m. Suddenly, every light came on and the ward was brightly lit, including the dormitories where patients slept. Sarah had not yet left the ward but walked quickly back, asking what was going on. Phil hadn't moved and sat there for a minute in disbelief as obviously neither of them had switched the lights on and would never do so, as it would wake up patients. It was also physically impossible to put them all on at once, unless there were 2 people in the different areas where the switches were flicking them on at the same time. All patients were in bed and no one else was on the ward. The electricians could not explain this phenomenon.

One evening, Brian and his colleague both noticed a blast of cold air he described as like an "arctic blast," whistling past them. He asked his seated colleague if she had felt it too. Both experienced it, but could find no reason for it. It was a warm summer evening. Sash windows only opened four inches and there was no wind. In the distance, a faint figure suddenly appeared and then seemed to dissolve.

Mark and his female colleague were sitting there one night when they both sensed someone or something behind them. Neither felt they could turn and look and, within a few seconds, the feeling subsided.

When Shelton Hospital had been closed for two years and was awaiting renovation by Shropshire Homes, I was lucky to visit twice with former colleagues, accompanied by a security guard Shaun, as part of the Shelton Heritage Project. Cheryl Pearce, Lorraine Fletcher and I went primarily to photograph it and add information to the Facebook page, "Shelton Hospital Community 1845-2012." The second time I went with 2 colleagues who hadn't worked in the main Shelton building but were part of the NHS Trust, one a secretary and the other a nurse. Both were also 'mediums' but as they want to keep that quiet, I will call them Sandra and Janice.

The fourth person was Lorraine Fletcher, who had an interest in the history of Shelton, having had a relative repeatedly admitted years before. She was also a very talented photographer. Lorraine has received awards from her work and runs "For the Love of Shrewsbury" and Shropshire Facebook pages and also provides photos for the designs of my book covers.

Sandra and Janice alerted us to many things around the hospital that were only known by those who had worked there. I didn't tell them ward names or whether they had been male or female, or any information on deceased staff or suicides, but they sensed things in a lot of detail.

As we entered the nurse's station on Beech Ward, it felt like we were walking through spider webs that touched our faces and hands. But despite its emptiness and it no longer being cleaned, there were no cobwebs. We even tried sweeping the fragile strands from our faces, only to find there were none. Sandra explained that those within the paranormal field believe that this tickling feeling results from being touched by a spirit using strings of ectoplasm. Also, from contact with the veil that separates the world of the living and the spirit world.

Leaving to walk down the long gallery, Sandra felt and sensed an elderly man holding on to her arm, playfully asking her not to leave. It was so strange to observe her turning to speak to him, unafraid, and going through the motions of gently removing his arm from hers. It was something no one else could see. As we moved on, both medium staff stopped abruptly and told us there was a woman stood at the bottom of the corridor near the bathroom and dormitory. Lorraine and

I could not see her, but it deterred us from going any further. As we turned back, a powerful smell of urine, which wasn't there before, emerged and it definitely wasn't any of us!

Two of my colleagues nursed patents who survived the fire. Liz and Katrina reported patients getting distressed decades later when reminded of it. One of these elderly ladies could see the front of Beech Ward from her room at The Redwoods Centre, built opposite, and which replaced Shelton. She had advanced dementia by then, but apparently stood screaming one day and they had to move her to a room on the other side of the building.

This chapter is in memory of all the female patients who sadly lost their lives on that fateful night, or later in hospital. Also, those who experienced trauma from their ordeal. Kind permission from group members Including Jackie Falconer, whose great Granny, Mary Ann Haycox, was one of many who didn't make it. When they found her walking home across the fields to Ludlow at the age of 82, they moved her to the locked ward. John Oswell, who worked as a domestic and nursing assistant at Shelton, also tragically lost his grandmother in the fire. He stated that he always felt her presence, as if she was watching over him on Beech Ward.

May all those who lost their lives rest in peace.

KateMcLanachan

The Great Fire

Beech Ward

CHAPTER 8

Staff Spirits

Chestnut Ward was originally 'Female 15,' and part of an extension eleven years after Shelton opened in 1856. They built it on the back of the hospital, along with Beech Ward above, as well as the new Rodney and Housman Wards. At the time of this ghost story, it was a mixed sex ward for patients with dementia.

Larry, a nursing assistant who has permitted me to use his name, was on night duty on Chestnut Ward and is sure the time was 3 a.m. He knew this, as he and his two colleagues had all just finished their individual one-hour breaks from midnight. They were all sitting quietly by the linen cupboard in the entrance to the dormitory area, when he looked up to see a lady standing outside the single bedroom opposite. When the staff nurse whispered, "don't move," he realised she had seen her too. The third colleague stared aghast, wide eyed and open mouthed. Larry's first thought, unsurprisingly, was that she must be a patient, even though a recent check showed them all to be asleep in bed in their night attire.

There was no possibility of her being a member of staff. They were all accounted for, and the nurse manager was a man. It couldn't be the patient in the side-room, as she was immobile and had cot sides up to prevent her from falling out. He described her as a small, older lady dressed in black and wearing a white apron.

Afterwards, trying to make sense of the vision, he likened her image to a female attendant he had seen in a photograph from the mid 1800s. Although she looked like a physical person, there was something unreal and old-fashioned about her motionless presence. She eventually slowly faded, becoming more and more transparent until she disappeared before their eyes. The other nursing assistant apparently ran towards the kitchen screaming and came out reciting the Bible and throwing salt over her shoulder.

He mentioned it to the ward Sister the next morning, and she just said, "Don't tell anyone, they won't want to work nights!"

During the mid to late nineteenth century, the female attendant's uniform comprised their own floor length black dresses worn under a long white pinafore and topped with a nurse's cap. Larry and his colleagues were not the only ones to encounter a long dead female attendant at Shelton Hospital.

Retired nurse, Marie, who has permitted me to use her first name, told me about her ghostly vision on Willow Ward. As you will know from previous chapters, Willow was a female dementia ward and has had many sightings of a 'grey lady.' It used to be called 'Laundry Ward' as had the big laundry building on the end and patients worked there using the new steam machinery from 1869, as well as knitting socks and making curtains. Patients here would have slept on 'Female Laundry Up,' that became Ash Ward above. Please refer to the Chapter 11- The History of Shelton, to see the name changes. It might intrigue the people who knew the hospital, remembering how the ward names have changed over the years.

Marie describes herself as someone who has been susceptible to the paranormal for as long as she can remember, telling me there were always "odd things going on at Shelton." The most memorable ones she shared are as follows. Whilst alone on night duty as a student nurse in 1981, Marie was quietly keeping herself busy in order to stay awake whilst her patients slept soundly. This was her first night working by herself. She dimmed all the lights, leaving only the office desk light on. She described having her head down writing reports, when suddenly she felt like she had company. Looking up through the office window at the far end of the ward, there was a lady sitting by the door in the corner on a low stool. Getting up to take her back to bed, Marie walked towards her, but as she approached, the lady just faded away.

Thinking she must have just imagined it, Marie walked back to the office, but once seated, the lady re-appeared in solid form, again in the corner. Trying to take in more details, she could see the lady was dressed in day clothes, not night attire. But the style of dress was more reminiscent of that seen in the last century rather than the 1980s. She had a plump figure and wore a long black skirt with a 'pinny' or apron over it and had a shawl around her shoulders. Her belt had a long chain with keys attached.

Marie said she was almost expecting, "to hear the chain and keys rattle as in horror films," but they didn't, as the lady was just silently sitting there smiling. Not feeling threatened, Marie carried on with her night duties, but every time she looked over, the lady was still sat there. As dawn approached, she went for a quick break outside to get some fresh air and, on return, the woman had disappeared completely. Even the stool had gone and she never saw her again.

The other strange occurrence happened on night duty on Darwin Ward, when Marie again was on her own. All the men were fast asleep with lights dimmed as usual. Darwin was originally 'Male D2 Up,' built in 1884, another later extension to the hospital. All the ground floor wards had either 'Male or Female' with a letter and number after it, and the ones above had the same, but with 'Up' on the end. Where brass light switches still existed, they stamped Ward names like A1 onto them. In 1945, there were 1000 patients in Shelton. The ground floors were then day areas and the first floors were dormitories, with beds crammed together.

Marie was working a night shift on Darwin Ward when it housed long-stay male patients. It was around 4 a.m. and she had just finished her work and was keeping quietly busy to stay awake. It was a sackable offence to sleep on duty, but is recognised as very difficult between the hours of 2-4 a.m. when most other people are asleep. With a cup of coffee and her knitting in hand, Marie settled down in an easy chair.

Marie had heard of night nurse paralysis but never experienced it. But it wasn't long before she found she was sitting in her chair, not really knowing if she was asleep or awake. She tried to move her arms and feet, but they felt like lead weights. Wondering what was happening, she suddenly smelt fresh pipe smoke. This was followed by someone gently stroking her left arm and saying to her in a Welsh accent, "Come on now, cariad, time to move." Cariad is a term of endearment used a lot in Wales, like you might call someone 'love.' After the touch and voice, Marie realised she had a male physical presence beside her.

"He was a little stocky fella, pipe in his hand, and I could see he was encouraging me to wake up and move myself. I managed to put my knitting down and shuffle my feet to get out of the chair." Marie still felt strange and, in her efforts to stand up, she thought the patient had gone back to bed. She needed to spend a penny and get another cup of coffee, but first went into the dormitory to see which patient was out of bed. Of course, everyone was fast asleep. As she walked back down the corridor, the night charge nurse came through the door.

"He checked everything was ok and off he went. Thank goodness I was awake," Marie said.

Her instinctive thought was that he was a 'lifer,' which was a term she used as well as an 'inmate.' She thought they had admitted the man there because of low intelligence, or what we would now call a learning difficulty. In fact, sadly, at one time these poor people were often called 'idiots' or 'imbeciles,' which are such derogatory terms nowadays. She said he was gentle and definitely of "Welsh farming stock", with a short, stocky, square build. She felt he was maybe nudging her, so she didn't get into trouble and felt his contact was an act of kindness. It is documented that many patients had jobs on the wards, such as cleaning, making tea and even helping to care for other patients. I like to think that perhaps he kept the lone night attendants' company and watched out for the matron doing her rounds.

Although Darwin Ward (Male D2 'Up') had back stairs and a fire escape, staff could reach it from Clive Ward by going up four steps. However, the door remained locked and only the staff used it. Clive ward was originally Male B1 'Up,' and before it closed, they renamed it Buildwas Ward.

Several staff on this ward have seen the apparition of a woman coming down Darwin's corridor and floating down the steps to Clive. Anyone who wanted a quiet break on their night shift on Clive Ward had to go up these steps to the first side-room on the left of the old Darwin Ward (closed for many years). However, they were renowned for not staying long or repeating the experience thanks to the sudden cold dip in temperature. This happened separately to Sarah and Kim, who kept their eyes tightly shut but felt dreadfully uneasy and not alone.

Two other staff, Anna and Philip, told me similar stories. Both had felt the air go icy cold, making them open their eyes only to see a woman glide past the window in the door. Philip said he could see his own breath before the room immediately became warm again after she passed.

Staff Nurse Lorna remembers a similar "odd moment", when she was lying on the sofa on a night shift break in the staff room along that same corridor, on the empty Darwin Ward. She said she had just closed her eyes when she heard a loud shriek at one end of the room and a "ridiculously icy breeze" pass over her. The room was typically very warm, with all the windows shut. Instinctively, she froze, too afraid to open her eyes until the temperature returned to normal. She then leapt up and ran out of the room and down the steps, so afraid that she left her mug and blanket behind.

Later, after they renamed the ward 'Buildwas,' a staff nurse called Chris, was sitting in the dining room, positioned to observe all corridors as patients slept. Hearing a noise, he looked up and noticed the shape of a female standing in the kitchen and assumed it was his co-worker making a drink. When his colleague appeared walking down from the opposite direction, he looked again, but the woman had disappeared. He went into the kitchen and noticed an old tea urn out on the side. It was an old-fashioned pot that he had remembered seeing in the back of a cupboard that was never used now. It could make tea for about 15 people, with milk and sugar often added before pouring. This was a very institutionalised, old way of providing communal tea.

Ellen, his colleague, was not surprised, as she had heard so many stories about the old female night attendant who patrolled the corridor above on Darwin Ward. The ward was open in the day for use as administration and management offices, and had a reputation for being spooky. The stories of her gliding through the door and down onto the ward below were well known. People describe the apparition as quite faint, and it's difficult to make out her clothes, but three staff members have told me they are certain she was a nurse or matron. They based this on her long dark dress that was not of this era and as this was the male side; they guessed it was staff.

A ghostly staff encounter really surprised me when, in 2014, we got to walk through the hospital after it had been empty for two years. The level of dilapidation and decay shocked us, as it had happened so quickly. With no heating or ventilation, the damp and mold had got in and paint and plaster were peeling off walls. The walls were wet and floors were surprisingly damp and slippery in places. Shelton was about to be renovated by Shropshire Homes. Cheryl and I were very familiar with the hospital, having worked there for many years.

The 24-hour security guards, including Shaun and John, reported many noises in the dead of night, from all over the empty hospital. They knew "urban explorers" had found a way in twice, but these loud, inexplicable noises often occurred during the 'witching hour.'

The second time when we went in with our two 'medium,' colleagues, I became convinced that they had psychic abilities after some experienced things they described and from what they saw and heard that night. As we walked through the deserted hospital, I remember feeling quite nostalgic as we entered Larch Ward. I had first worked there when newly qualified, on day and night duty, aged 22. It was an acute female admission ward, taking patients from the Telford area. Later, they converted it into the medical records department. I hadn't worked on all the wards by any means, even as a student, and although I knew most of their names, I hadn't told the two mediums the names of wards I had worked on.

Suddenly, one of the 'medium' staff stopped and turned around. "There's a man here who knows you, Kate, and wants to say hello to you." My face must have been a picture. I was not expecting that at all. I couldn't see or hear anything but remember saying, "Who is it?" Of course, my colleague didn't know, but when she described his approximate age and rank on the ward, I knew immediately that it was a colleague who had sadly passed away over a decade ago. I won't name him or give more details, as his family may find it distressing. I'm sorry if he hasn't passed over and hope he is at peace.

I was 100% sure she felt the spirits of the deceased. When she then paused outside the side-room nearest to the office, she touched her neck and said, "someone died in this room from strangulation." She could feel a tightness around her throat and a deep sadness prevail. "She regretted it, but it was too late and no one would hear her." I had never forgotten something I learned on arriving on duty at 7:45 a.m. nearly 30 years ago, one dark winter's morning. A patient we were all very fond of had unexpectedly hanged herself from the curtain rail in the night, in this very side-room.

The last ghostly staff story I wanted to include was when a retired colleague told me about her time living in a house in The Crescent in the early 1980s. These were the staff houses in front of Shelton, along with The Circle. They had boarded one house up and left it unused for some time. She was told there was nothing else available, so asked about renting this one. Mary, whose name I have changed, was desperate to find somewhere to live. Nobody could recall the reason for the house not being rented out for so long. Reluctantly, maintenance got it ready for her with a quick coat of paint and numbered it 12a. She could not understand why the numbers ran 11, 12, 12a, and 14, and no one else seemed to know either. She guessed it was just because number 13 was unlucky.

Mary moved in with her partner and son and enjoyed living there. They took no notice of odd noises and bumps in the night, assuming it was noisy neighbours. As time went on, they came home to find the television on and noticed lights switching on and off, but they laughed it off. Paranormal experiences never bothered them. Unfortunately, the atmosphere would start to change and turn nasty when she was getting ready for bed at night in the bathroom. The door would jam so Mary couldn't get out or it just swung open. Once the toothbrush glass, which was inside a holder, smashed on the floor and toothpaste smeared over the mirror. Mary knew her young son could not possibly have done this. This happened to Mary and no one else in the house.

Then one evening, whilst soaking in the large cast iron bath, she suddenly felt the full weight of a body on top of her. Something held her down, hands around her throat, pushing her under the water. She fought, terrified, struggling with all her might to free herself. Hooking her toes around the chain, she pulled the plug out. The water drained and everything went back to normal. Feeling unsettled, she began enquiring about the history of the house and the reason for its long period of vacancy.

No one seemed to know for sure, but apparently a young physiotherapist (occupation changed to protect identity) who had previously rented the house had a tragic love story. He was said to have fallen in love with a young nurse against the wishes of his family, who had planned for him to have an arranged marriage. According to rumours, his family disowned him and he faced disgrace. As a result, he was said to have taken sleeping tablets and drowned himself in the bath.

CHAPTER 9

SECRET SPACES, ATTICS & CELLARS

"We ask only to be reassured about the noises in the cellar and the window that should not have been open".
—T.S. Eliot, "The Family Reunion"—

This chapter looks at the secrets Shelton held in the early days, and what went on behind closed doors which may have left an imprint on the physical structure. According to the Stone Tape theory, every trauma and joy somehow locks itself in the walls, leaving behind imprints that manifest as hauntings. The theory suggests that residual ghosts are not intelligent beings but rather energy imprints.

Another explanation for paranormal experiences in former asylums is that the surroundings may have absorbed years of isolation and despair, and sometimes the living can feel those emotions and experience strange occurrences. Some believe they can detect in the atmosphere the lost souls that cannot rest in peace or move on. Could it be a product of long suffering and distress that occurred because of the past, outdated, ineffective and often harmful treatments? Practices that were accepted during their era as being revolutionary.

So, who were the first people admitted to Shelton? Many came from pauper workhouses, families unable to cope, prisons and the streets. Before they made purpose-built asylums, only the rich could afford to put relatives into 'private madhouses.' In the mid 1800s, patients entered purpose-built accommodation which supported a humane attitude towards mental healthcare. The moral treatment system was a fresh approach aimed at treating people like human beings and frowned upon shackles, chains, and barbaric treatment. It did not last though, as asylums became overcrowded.

Visitors and staff have reported inexplicable feelings of sadness, unease and dramatic temperature changes invading the hospital. Spectral beings who walked the wards and basements, hiding in shadows, pacing aimlessly or walking purposefully, repeating their old routines. Some were opening and closing doors, banging or throwing objects and security, like Shaun heard toilets flush on empty wards. There were disembodied voices heard: crying, laughing, shouting, screaming, and whispering. A sense of feeling watched, hearing footsteps, seeing glowing lights and floating orbs, and sudden feelings of dread and depression.

There are books and social media videos on empty 'Lunatic Asylums,' that unfortunate former name, that depicts them as macabre. Such as this headline: "Horrifying ghost in hospital gown claimed to have been captured on camera at creepy old Welsh Asylum," in Wales Online by reporter John Cooper. A believer reads the article and a sceptic scrolls past. Unfortunately, the fear of asylums runs deep in western culture. Most asylum narratives have stigmatized the mentally ill and psychiatric care, leading to people being afraid to seek help.

A sceptic might suggest that if a person expects a place to be haunted, particularly an old mental hospital, then they may feel uneasy. If someone tells us a location is haunted and shares ghost stories, we are more likely to report freaky experiences. One could feel watched or followed, experience shivers and sense drops in temperature. Also, paranormal believers are allegedly more susceptible to such suggestions than sceptics.

During the redevelopment of Shelton to apartments, the builders often reported hearing children's voices. Paul, who delivered materials to the Shropshire Homes site while the construction was going on, was told a few strange stories by the men. While working in a basement room, a 'chippy' (carpenter) heard a high-pitched scream that startled him. It made him jump so high that he hit his own thumb, breaking it. With no one in sight, yet the noise directly behind him, he was terrified. He scrambled up the stairs on all fours and dived straight through the open window, refusing to go back in there alone.

When Shelton was closing, Marie helped with the research into its history, spending several days at the Shropshire Archives Repository. She examined old records to learn about the history of patient care throughout the years. She was specifically interested in their age, the reason for admission, where they came from and the treatment they received. In 1912, a 6-year-old boy was admitted to Shelton from Llanfyllin Workhouse, near Lake Vyrnwy in North Wales. The Matron deemed him as 'impudent of mind' and refusing to 'toe the line', so once in Shelton, they assigned the 'toughest male warder' to oversee him.

Following his story as much as she could, Marie discovered they kept the child isolated for six weeks, with only this warder permitted to see to him. After being released back to the workhouse, his notes stated the warder had successfully "broken his spirit," causing him to "no longer be impudent and comply with doing a full day's work." This young child's only 'offence' was reportedly that each time the Matron walked across the quadrangle he would turn the water tap on, press his finger against the spout, and squirt water over her.

It's upsetting to think about what physical and emotional abuse this young child must have endured from the cruel attendant. To 'break one's spirit,' you have to destroy a person's self-esteem and take away their joy in life, traumatising them so that all sense of self-worth is diminished. Could this be the child the construction workers heard, held down below ground floor level?

Another time, a window fitter said he saw an elderly lady walk right past him wearing Victorian clothing that, he was sure, was an old nurse's uniform. Her movements were soundless, and she stared purposefully ahead as if unaware of him. As his eyes followed her walking, she gradually faded until she disappeared. Down in the cellars, Craig, who was working on the hospital conversion, frequently experienced strange noises and the lights would flicker on and off. Working down there on his own, he always looked up, expecting to see another workman, but there was never anybody else there.

One builder reported seeing a little girl in the cellar before she just disappeared. Despite witnessing her vanish, he searched for her, convinced she must be a colleague's daughter who had got lost visiting the site. Yet on reflection, despite such a brief sighting, he said he knew deep down she was not a modern child or of this world.

On the photographic tour of the empty Shelton, Janice, our medium colleague, whose name I changed, became terrified when we went down the steps into the old underground area opposite the hall. She had to run back up quickly as she felt very nauseous, having picked up on palpable fear and distress. She felt something very unpleasant had taken place there. Her fellow medium colleague, Sandra, could stay down in the damp, dark room, lit only by our torches. Sensing evil, she strongly surmised it was a place where many years before, some terror-stricken, distressed person had suffered repeatedly at the hands of another in power.

It made us wonder if someone had taken vulnerable young women below floor level, under duress, terrified of the consequences of refusal and aware that they were unlikely to be believed and had no choice but to submit to abuse. Rob, a former colleague, reminded that they kept the photocopier down there when it was the only one in the hospital. He felt the atmosphere was very eerie and remembered seeing old cells down there with chains fixed on the walls. They had not sealed these off at the time.

There was also a tragic story, told to me some 30 years ago by a much older colleague, regarding a now deceased patient. When she was in her mid-60s, the patient disclosed that someone had raped her during her admission to Shelton when she was 16 years old. She had a mild learning disability, and she stated that someone had sexually abused her throughout her young life. Additionally, her siblings mercilessly bullied her, mistakenly believing that all the attention she received at home meant that she was their "father's favourite."

The nurse talked to a Consultant Psychiatrist, also in his sixties, about her claims, and he was sadly not surprised at all. He remembered, as a young doctor at Shelton, that there was a male charge nurse, now long deceased, whom two young female patients accused of this heinous act. He allegedly threatened both with ECT if they refused or told anyone. As there was no evidence, and it was their word against his, the doctor believed they took no action other than to move the nurse to "the back wards." This implied they moved him to long-stay wards with patients with either dementia or severe mental illness.

Historic complaints about the abuse of power were reportedly around complaints of wrongful confinement and exploitation once held under lock and key. Many unhappy people over the first century as a 'lunatic asylum' will have found themselves on locked wards with no rights to refuse treatment and many never left the hospital.

Since the early asylum days, attendants, nursing and medical staff were in daily contact with patients suffering from delusions and hallucinations that can disrupt perception of reality. The risks have always been that a patient could convincingly allege an assault by a caregiver that had not taken place. What may have been just as common was that a staff member could assault a patient whose accusations would be dismissed. Regarded as a false product of the person's mental condition.

My contact in Shropshire Homes described finding blocked off rooms and corridors in the basement, with cell like spaces that had chains on the walls. One room had what looked like electrical devices similar to vintage car battery chargers. If you look at images of the Electric Shock Therapy machines used by the Victorians, they could be easily mistaken for car chargers or boosters.

Janice, our medium colleague, felt drawn to climb up some steps into an attic when walking around the empty building. There was a chair at the top and, after sitting on it, she felt something was strongly trying to keep her there. Sandra had to coax her down because fear and unease had frozen her. Talking to old colleagues, we wonder if this was above the old Cedar Millington Ward's bedrooms on the first floor. From what they described, it was likely, but none of this group was familiar with the old ward names. Staff working on "Cedar Mill," like Neil, often experienced an "odd sensation" when walking underneath the hatch.

I remember working on Cedar Mill Ward as a third-year student nurse when it was a mixed sex rehabilitation ward. We had to go upstairs to the rooms to do checks at nights and wake patients before breakfast. I always felt it had an "eerie feeling" around the area above the bedroom corridor, where there was a locked attic space. There have been rumours for years about seclusion areas up there, although they could simply be ventilation shafts with cold spots underneath.

Under Cedar Millington, there were rows of baths that remained there for years after they had stopped being used for hydrotherapy. This is not the same as we think of it in our era. As described in Chapter 7, they had a grislier use after the great fire on Beech Ward in 1968. Then, they laid out bodies on top of the boards as there was no space in the mortuary.

Teresa, her name also changed, shared her story on the Shelton Facebook page. Previously, when she was a

community patient, she had to use the back stairs from the allegedly 'haunted' Haughmond Ward to go up to what was then 'Berrington Suite.' This was then where the Eating Disorder team was based. She described always feeling like she was being watched and someone was walking with her, saying, "It scared the living daylights out of me."

Retired porter Peter, who started working at Shelton in 1971, remembers that they didn't have a restroom for breaks at first. Instead, they used a couple of chairs down the cellar where they had their lunch. The "creepy" room was at the bottom of the ramp leading to Rodney and Sidney Wards.

Another retired porter, renamed Roger, contacted me with a story and asked to be kept anonymous, but claimed to have had two terrifying experiences in the restroom. He always kept it to himself for fear of being teased. After the second experience, he vowed never to go down there alone again, finding other areas to smoke or take his breaks. He became a regular visitor on Hill Ward, as he could always get a cup of tea there and have a chat with his favourite staff.

Roger saw what he described as a "shadow man." It started one day, after two light bulbs shattered at the same time. As he searched the cupboard for spare bulbs, he saw a dark humanoid figure lurking in the corner. It moved left and right like it was captured in a confined space, and this caught his eye. He backed out of the door, not taking his eyes off it, and ran up the ramp. A colleague spotted him and asked what was wrong, as the terror was written all over his face. Thinking on his feet, he quickly came up with an explanation. He informed his colleague about three rats fighting in the room, and that he had had to go to run to stores to get some poison because he had nearly been bitten.

The second time, he was still very wary about being alone in the room, but had popped in to get his coat as it was raining when the door slammed behind him. This time, the 'shadow man' was standing against the closed door, not moving. It was taller this time and very thin and, despite having no facial features, it somehow felt menacing and was watching him. Roger found himself trapped with no other exit and he noticed that the room temperature had dropped considerably. He could see his own breath. His heart was beating fast, but he stood still, too afraid to take his eyes off it. Suddenly it seemed to float down under the closed door like a sheet of paper. Roger's next dilemma was whether it was waiting on the other side, but the lights started flickering, so he made his mind up and ran up the ramp for the second time, never returning alone.

Caroline was based in the Pharmacy in the newer extension back in 2008. She didn't see or hear anything there, but felt something unsettling below the area of the ramps leading to the dining room. She hated using this route to deliver medication to the wards. If there was nobody about, she ran, hoping nobody would see her. Could it have been 'the shadow man,' lurking there still?

We have a photograph taken of the lower ramp leading to the stores and porter's room, with a possible strange ghostly spectre that appears to be standing at the bottom. Some people think it is a white sheet hanging on a hook. Whilst others see a hooded figure or a woman leaning back as if trying to stand out of sight. Perhaps it is the grey lady in her off-white nightdress?

Imagine a secret ward, discovered boarded up behind a false wall in the basement areas of the hospital. Although my main Shropshire Homes contact doesn't remember seeing it, rumours from others renovating those areas are that it may very well have existed. When knocking down walls, they found two antiquated rooms, sealed doors, and bricked up corridors. Like opening a tomb, they uncovered entire areas previously unrevealed and not on the maps. They found small cell like spaces and larger empty rooms behind doors on either side of long passages. Unlike wards closed in Shelton's last decade, these were full of antique dust and thick spiders' webs. The few objects found inside were of no monetary value and little historic interest, but were from a bygone era.

So, was this entire hidden floor below ground level an abandoned old ward from the 1800s? Disused for over a century? Its resemblance to a hospital ward was almost unrecognisable in the absence of abandoned medical equipment. Or could it have just been a large storage area no longer required and so shut away? One unlikely theory is that they used it for 'royalty' requiring respite in the country or high-ranking town's people or ministers of the church. Another possibility, looking at what occurred elsewhere in Britain, is that it was holding cells and areas for the most unpredictable and dangerous patients. With a narrow gallery, no windows or fresh air, and before electricity, it would have been cold and dingy.

When Shelton opened, it would be another century before medication replaced physical restraint. Early hope that the facility would bring cures soon evaporated. It became a place of confinement for the most seriously mentally ill patients. They constantly added new wings and extensions on the back of the building as numbers rose and more people were certified 'insane.' As more people arrived, fewer ever left and numbers increased from just over 100 on opening to 1000 by 1900.

Newly arriving patients entered a well decorated, comfortable foyer, rather like a hotel. Once they were beyond the double doors, they faced a warren of corridors with stairs to wards with long galleries, day rooms and nightingale dormitories. They would see padded cells and impersonal communal bathrooms and toilets.

Sir George Paget (1809-1892) described the asylum as "the most blessed manifestation of true civilization the world can present." 130 years later, one historian described them as "museums for the collection of the unwanted."

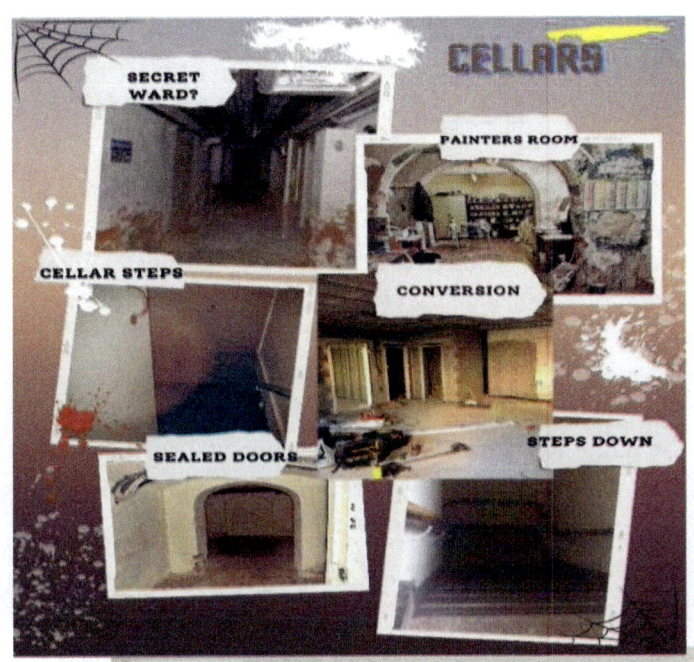

CHAPTER 10

THE MORTUARY

"I have pleasures, and passions, but the joy of life is gone. I am going under: the morgue yawns for me. I go and look at my zinc-bed there. After all, I had a wonderful life, which is, I fear, over."
—Oscar Wilde—

Originally known as a 'dead- house', 'Rose Cottage' was a common name for a mortuary used by hospital staff. It was to avoid upsetting other patients who may overhear them talking on the ward. Once a doctor officially pronounced somebody dead, porters would take the patient to 'Rose Cottage.' They sometimes referred to the deceased as 'Rosie.'

In Victorian times, they established a regime of presumed consent to dissection, meaning they did not always get relatives' consent to post-mortem. Additionally, many older long-stay patients had long lost any contact with their families. The institutionalised dead only avoided dissection if they or their relatives made a formal objection during life, or soon after death. In 1832, if a pauper's body remained unclaimed for burial for 2 days, authorities could dissect the corpses for pathological research or sell them to licensed anatomy schools for medical practice and teaching. The need for medical students to supply their own bodies led to the existence of body snatchers. As a result, iron cages we sometimes placed over graves to deter thieves. Some dissection on site took place in attempts to clarify cause of death or in the wider pursuit of 'psychiatric knowledge.'

Patients died for a variety of reasons, although some after living to a ripe old age, having had every need cared for. They received good food, warmth and basic medicine, not always affordable to the public outside the asylum. But we know that despite the hospital trying to keep people safe, many succumbed to death by their own hand, such as hanging, drowning, poisoning or fatal self-inflicted injury.

The original mortuaries, or dead-houses, had a well-ventilated room with top windows. There was a separate room or area, called a 'chapel of rest,' where the family could view their deceased relative. Also, a dissection room, a cold room used before the invention of refrigeration and a 'museum' for casts which were taken off the face shortly after death. Later, if a post-mortem took place, they took casts of both the interior and exterior 'bony arch.'

Years later, one of our Shelton Facebook page members, a retired nurse, informed us her stepfather-in-law installed the first refrigeration systems in Shelton's mortuary. Before this, in the 1800s, they used ice boxes and insulated wooden cabinets. Despite using ice, decomposing corpses still emitted an odour described as rank, pungent and nauseating, mixed with a tinge of sickening sweetness. Mortuaries were built away from the main living areas. There would be one or more slabs to examine the deceased, made of slate and later metal. Inventions such as scales, gas jets, microscopes and a rose douche came later.

Shelton did not have a burial ground, so all unclaimed deceased denied private family burials went by cart to local parish churchyards and received pauper graves. Sadly, it is doubtful that they even provided paupers with a coffin and, if they did, it would be very plain and basic. It could be several weeks or months before those bodies used for medical use were laid to rest. Some were anonymously buried in multiple plots and with missing body parts.

The area around the mortuary has looked very different over the years. In my day, in the late 1980s, the mortuary had recently closed and became the multigym. Physiotherapists like Jackie and Lesley ran this. Staff could use the equipment at night. That is, if they dared to go in there in the dark on their breaks!

Sam trained 18 months before me and remembers it was open then, in about 1986. She and another student who lived in the nurses' block investigated it one night. They climbed on a wall to peer through a window. Although they saw nothing, they managed to scare each other witless and ran all the way back. Some staff remember a domestic on Willow Ward whose job was also to clean the mortuary. Someone accidentally locked her in once and she was reportedly, "never the same again." In those days, people didn't carry mobile phones and there was no land line installed. The mortuary was on the left of the estate's restroom. I asked Kevin from estates if there was ever any paranormal activity. He said he had heard nothing, but "Mind you, the estates workers were all spooky, anyway!" Walking past the old mortuary at Shelton, security officers situated there before renovation started reported having small stones thrown at their legs.

Jane recalls when you had a death at Shelton, you went to Benbow ward to collect the last offices pack. In nurse training, they taught you how to perform the care of the deceased with dignity. They would ask hospital porters to fetch the covered wheeled mortuary trolley to collect the body. They performed final care of the person with such respect. When Peter was a porter in the 1970s, the trolley had a fibreglass coffin on top. They reportedly had to use fire escapes to remove the body from the ward, so as not to distress the living.

Woman staff were called upon to accompany a female body to the mortuary. This was, unfortunately, because of the risk of necrophilia, sexual intercourse with the deceased. Although thought to be extremely rare, once discovered to have taken place, safeguards were put firmly in place. Terry recalled helping to lay out the bodies of patients who had passed away and dressing them in a linen shroud. Phil attended two post mortems there in the presence of a Police Officer, pathologist and coroner. He stayed on his feet but will never forget the experience.

One nurse, who wishes to remain anonymous, remembers they used to help take patients down on a big metal trolley he called the "death trolley." Years later, he was working on New House, an old building at the front of the hospital and at the time a drug and alcohol detoxification unit. The mortuary was long gone, and ambulances or a funeral director took the deceased to the general hospital if a postmortem was required. One night, he was in the office with his back to the window when he heard metal clanging in the distance, which got louder as it approached the building. Sounding like a trolley, rattling and with the distinct sound of metal caster wheels wobbling and swivelling back and forth. It was very loud and creaky. It eventually stopped outside the office window, but as it was pitch black, he rushed to the back door and opened it. The security light was on and he walked around the building and surrounding area, but there was nothing outside. He was "freaked," but smoked a quick cigarette and went back inside, hearing nothing more.

Paul (requested name changed) once got called to take some false teeth to the mortuary chapel of rest. The deceased person was without them and his family were coming to pay their respects. He had to collect the key from the porter's lodge and remembers its enormous size, likening it to a castle key. When he got there, he let himself in and, switching on the lights, he approached the body to put the teeth in. He carefully pulled back the sheet to reveal the face and the 'corpse' sat up from the slab and said, "have you got my teeth?"

Simon, who nursed at Shelton, once got locked in by a colleague, as a prank in the middle of the night. They had just dropped someone off when the lights went out and the door slammed. He had to wait for about an hour until his giggling colleague returned. Fran, a nursing assistant, also got locked in by a colleague once as a joke. The porters were on strike and she and nurse Terry had to take down an elderly lady who had passed away. It almost scared her to death! Nurse Denise also got locked in once by 2 male colleagues.

The late Mr Les Mills, a nurse tutor for many decades, told all students the story of a body that fell off the trolley once in the heavy snow and how they struggled to find it! They used to lift bodies onto a stretcher that they could use separately from the wheeled base. I think that night someone had not secured it properly to the trolley. Nurse Mike remembers lifting a body to slide it into the mortuary fridge. He stood at over 6 feet 4 inches, while his female colleague, Helen, barely reached 5 feet. During that time, the trolleys didn't come with adjustable heights, and the top fridge was the only empty one. Helen stepped up on a stool as they lifted the tiny woman's body onto the shelf to match Mike's tall frame and share the weight. As he stepped back and Helen jumped down, she saw the body's tagged big right toe wiggle. They rushed the patient back to the ward, only for the doctor to declare she was 'definitely dead'. The doctor explained that 'Cadaveric spasms' are when the body twitches as muscles and joint tighten before rigor mortis.

Now converted into a bungalow, 'Rose Cottage,' is owned by a lovely lady. She has invited me to have a look around in exchange for information about the original place. I look forward to taking her up on her offer!

'Unifashions' was the patient's clothes shop where patients could purchase reasonably priced clothes. It was next to the mortuary, and Amanda worked there at one time. She saw nothing, but she said that the back storeroom had an eerie feel to it and she heard odd noises from inside. Amanda worked with Cherie, but would have worked some days there alone. At these times, she would draw the curtains as the windows on the left of the storeroom looked out over a small yard leading to the mortuary. There were also two doors leading out to the yard, one from the storeroom, and a fire escape door from the shop. The 'scary things' always occurred when Amanda worked alone, but she knew that with old buildings, you often hear every creak and pop when there's no one else present. Amanda also worked in the Laundry and always put the lights on before putting her head through the door, afraid that the shadows would reveal an apparition lurking there.

I remember even in the late 1980s that all the long stay male and female wards had generic clothing on rails. You picked an outfit you thought would fit for them. We had a budget for Willow Ward and bought a whole rail of floral polyester dressers that hung at the back of the dorm. We picked a dress for patients whom we helped get changed from this communal rail, although some had their own clothes. I remember choosing a dress and matching cardigan I thought would suit a particular patient. They had advanced dementia and could not communicate, but responded to a warm, caring approach. As newly qualified staff, we did as more experienced staff taught us and rarely questioned accepted practices unless you saw something clearly wrong. But we were becoming more aware of the effects of institutionalisation and the need to respect personal dignity.

Most long-stay wards made up bundles of clothes for patients, trying to ensure waist sizes and trouser lengths would fit. Kas said sometimes that you had to make a choice whether a patient looked better in a big waist with leg length to fit or waist to fit and shorter legs. There was a lot of fighting amongst male patients for a working pair of braces. Katrina said Rodney Ward had an entire room where they made up 3 bundles for each patient. The staff dressed older ladies in dresses, with splits up the back for easier dressing and increased comfort because of their contracted legs and arms. Double bathrooms with just a curtain in between existed to bathe 2 patients at once. Jane remembers some wards having 3 baths in a row.

Kevin confirmed that the Recreation Department, known as 'The Rec', was on the right, next to the Unifashions clothes shop. The Rec offered activities like bingo, films, games, table tennis, badminton, football, and skittles. They gained a pool table after Charge Nurse John Roach ran the Telford marathon to raise money to purchase one.

Years before, The Rec was a tailor's shop where patients worked under supervision. At one time, the cobbler's shop was there too, repairing boots and another room where patients made candles. The women patients sewed and darned on the ward, also making curtains and tablecloths. Many were from Laundry Ward that later became Willow. Much later, it became 'Mrs Paddock's Suits'. They gave each of the male staff a fully fitted, made to measure suit and uniform dresses handmade for female staff too. In later years, Mrs Paddock moved to the Linen Room, part of the laundry.

The late Roger Ellis, a respected former charge nurse, ran a workshop at The Rec, with the "heavy gang," a group of male patients considered 'bad lads' who were some of the most difficult male patients, making rustic furniture and paving slabs. The butcher's shop was next to the general stores directly underneath Clive Ward courtyard with a ramp leading to it. Waste food used to be collected by the pig man. I remember in the 1980s scraping plates of unfinished food into a wide lidded white bucket called the 'pig bin' by staff but was told that it didn't go to the pigs anymore. The name had stuck over generations.

KateMcLanachan

CHAPTER 11

THE HISTORY OF SHELTON

Before Shelton Hospital existed, the local 'lunatic' population went to the Kingsland Workhouse, also known as the 'House of Industry,' overlooking the River Severn. The building now houses the prestigious Shrewsbury School. My first book, "The Workhouse Almanac ~A Story of Shrewsbury," is a novel I wrote about these times, with local facts and fiction intertwined.

1841: A committee formed to look at plans to build a purpose-built Lunatic Asylum for the county. This was happening all over Britain, and it became compulsory in 1845 to house 'pauper lunatics and idiots', meaning mentally ill and learning-disabled people, unable to meet the costs of their own care.

Location: Bicton Heath, Shrewsbury

Built: 1843-1845 on a 15-acre plot of land in the parish of St. Julian, set apart from mainstream society

Principal Architects: George Gilbert Scott and William B Moffatt.

Cost: £17,000.

Layout: Wards were symmetrical corridors with the segregation of males and females.

Capacity: 60 patients, however, 104 were waiting for admission when Shelton opened. **Opened**: 18 March 1845

Closed: 13 September 2012

Status: The main building survives and is Grade II listed. In 2014, Shropshire Homes renovated and converted it into private homes renamed as 'Leighton Park.' It now comprises around 159 houses, bungalows and apartments within the traditional buildings, plus several luxury detached houses in the grounds. I believe they converted the chapel into 4 homes.

Leighton Park is named after Sir Baldwin Leighton, a local dignitary who chose the location back in 1842. He had visited other lunatic asylums across the country to set a standard for the care and conditions.

Significant Dates:

The construction of Shelton Hospital took place in 1843/45, initially as a much smaller building with the capacity to take only 60 patients.

1845: Originally named 'Shropshire and Wenlock Borough Lunatic Asylum', during its first half century, it underwent a sizeable extension with new wards built behind the main entrance and along the front.

1855/6: Construction of two more female and male ward blocks. Another purchase included over 15 acres of farmland, including farm buildings. Shelton became quite self-sufficient and the second cheapest hospital in the UK to operate.

1858: The building of a chapel behind the main building.

1859: The building of an alehouse under the main hall. Beer was less than 1% alcohol and only given to "real working patients and by medical order." This implied farm and garden workers mainly, not laundry, kitchen or domestic duty staff.

1869: A steam laundry and the adjacent 'Laundry Ward' built on the female side of the hospital.

1884: 5 new wards constructed, a superintendent's house, extension of the administration offices, and the building of the main hall. They extended the laundry and kitchen. The asylum land received an addition of a cricket ground.

1888: The county council now responsible for the asylum. Previously funded by private donations. Treating both pauper and private patients, the latter paid for their own care. Many others who could pay went to private asylums like Kingsland in Shrewsbury and Church Stretton.

1905: An isolation unit named Hawthorn Ward built due to an outbreak of Tuberculosis (TB), which claimed the lives of 167 people between 1905-1910.

1927: A villa purchased in 1927 to accommodate 40 working patients.

1930: Oxon Hall purchased as an annex for long-stay patients.

1940/41: 'The Copthorne and Shelton Emergency Hospital' huts built to care for up to 400 war casualties.

1947: At its peak, the hospital had 1027 patients.

1948: A Regional Hospital Board takes over the duty of providing an asylum under the NHS, and the title changes to 'Shelton Hospital.'

1968: The fire on Beech ward claimed the lives of 21 patients, and 3 the following day, prompted the development of plans to move away from long-stay hospitals. Rehabilitation wards, shorter admissions, community nurses, and day centres opened as part of 'care in the community.'

2012: There were approximately 200 patients accommodated at Shelton Hospital before it closed. The Redwoods Centre, a new £45 million mental health village, opened on adjacent land. The 10-acre site has four buildings and 7 wards containing 116 beds. It is part of a 50-year plan to modernise mental health care provision.

Notable Staff

Dr Henry Johnson 1845 was the first medical visitor to the new Shropshire 'Lunatic' Asylum. He was also a medic at the Royal Salop Infirmary (St. Mary's Place, Shrewsbury), inspector of the 'House of Industry' at Kingsland (Workhouse), and physician to the County Gaol.

Dr Richard Oliver 1845-1863 - The first Chief Medical Superintendent. His wife Sophia was the Matron. He had his own house and garden detached from the main building. The rules were that he had to "live in" and give the whole of his time to the duties of his office. There was a Welsh slate memorial plaque in the Chapel dedicated to him.

Dr Arthur Strange 1872-1902 - appointed as the fourth superintendent of 'Salop and Montgomery County Lunatic Asylum' in 1872. He lived on site in his house with wife Emma and their 7 children. There was a covered walkway from his house 'Plas Meddyg', to the main hospital, Male 2 (Rowans) to keep him dry on his daily visits to the wards.

Dr Strange was active in encouraging outdoor activities for patients, including sport, gardening and farming, as well as music when inside. He dedicated his life to the asylum, putting all his energy into it, modernising it, and always speaking up in defense of it. After a long illness, Dr Strange passed away at the hospital aged 58, from meningitis. There is a stained-glass window dedicated to him in the Chapel.

Dr Stanley Hughes 1913 - previously in charge of Denbigh Asylum in North Wales. He made Shelton the second cheapest UK asylum to run after Denbigh. Self-sufficient as it used patient's labour to run the farm and the asylum.

Dr John Barker 1966 – a psychiatrist working in Shelton Hospital who established the Premonitions Bureau. The purpose of his setup was to examine individuals who had foreseen accidents and incidents before they happened, with the potential for prevention. He became interested after receiving many reports of premonitions of the disaster at Aberfan, a Welsh mining village on 21 October 1966. He studied the possibility of something he called 'pre-disaster syndrome.' This related to his interest in the paranormal and a led to a proposal that premonitions should be a valid subject for modern psychiatry.

Dr Barker, known by Sam Knight, author of "The Premonitions Bureau," (published 2022) as 'The Psychiatrist Who Believed People Could Tell the Future.' 97% of the predictions sent to John at Shelton Hospital, to the Bureau, did not come true. Only 3% of the predictions were accurate and Barker, aged only 44, found his own predicted death fell in that minority. A friend who had accurately predicted a plane crash (Cyprus 1966) with exactly 124 casualties, foresaw John's death and warned him, but it was too late to prevent his brain embolism.

Dr Littlejohn, the Medical Superintendent at the time, had not supported further time or research spent on John's work. Regrettably, there was no forewarning to prevent the terrible fire at Shelton in 1968.

Dr David Enoch 1962 - Another young psychiatrist who worked closely with John Barker. Requesting lockers for patients to store their possessions, spare clothes, and encouraging them to get out of bed and pursue activities, he made many improvements. He was also instrumental in phasing out 'straight ECT', which was originally given without drugs. He and Dr John barker studied rarer conditions like Munchausen's syndrome and many more, which later formed a classic textbook in 1967 by Enoch called "Some Uncommon Psychiatric Syndromes."

Dr Littlejohn retired 1975 - the last Medical Superintendent. Retired nurse Vivian's dad worked at Shelton from 1938 to 1968 and had great respect for him.

Dr Thomas- Staff remember him on his ward rounds putting left over food in his white jacket pockets. Following this, he then gave food parcels to his "old dears" in his clinics. After the beer rations were cut, he spoke up and accurately predicted the increase in medicines. People knew him as "Dr Tom," and he was reputed for always making time for staff and patients.

Dr James Flowerdew- "Jimmie" was very popular with staff who recall him as "a legend." Our Shelton group remember how sociable he was, inviting staff around to his house for meals and drinks and he went to the retired nurse Alison's wedding. He was a consultant for the rehabilitation wards. He moved to Scotland, where he continued to work as a psychiatrist for many years.

Dr Brian Boettcher - wrote a published article on 'Cannabis Psychosis,' which references his time at Shelton. Researchers around the world widely used his findings.

There were many more psychiatrists and nurses whom I worked with in the 1980s until the present day, who I believe made some revolutionary changes to patient care and treatment. They helped bring about the closure of the old asylum, with care moving into the community and the prescribing of medication with less side-effects. In my time, I would say drugs like Clozapine intended for 'treatment resistant Schizophrenia' had a dramatic impact on reducing patients' symptoms. I saw this firsthand with patients I worked with in the community. It is notable that the increasing use of talking therapies in combination with medication has proved more effective than medication alone for most mental disorders.

Asking the Shelton Hospital Facebook group which psychiatrists stood out in their mind, we came up with a lot of names. We share some wonderful memories of working with great ward teams with some amazing doctors.

These include in no particular order:

Dr David Myers, Dr Norman Cocks, Dr David Bevington, Dr Patrick Campbell, Dr Sue Linford, Dr Gary Hosty, Dr Kevin Nicholls, Dr Sarah Lyle, Dr Philippa Walker, Dr Eleanor Adams, Dr Dennis, Dr Locke, Dr Ita Durkin, Dr Sally Burgess, Dr Anil Kumar, Dr Peter Everett, Dr Chris Murphy, Dr Ken Hughes, Dr Gareth Hughes, Dr Verma, Dr Sajeev Kshemendran, Dr Amrit Singh, Dr Keron Fletcher, Dr Vinni Chengapa, Dr David Rice, Dr Martin Bassett, Dr Tony Elliot, Dr Martin Deahl, Dr Simon Smith, Dr Alan Otter, Dr Claus Langmack, Dr Steve Novick, Dr Nick Swift, Dr Lehee, Dr Wasi Mohammad, Dr Hall, Dr Jimmie Flowerdew, Dr Thomas and Dr Littlejohn.

Early on, staff kept the asylum's complex running almost self-sufficiently and included:

❖ **Medical Superintendent and wife, often the Matron**

❖ **Assistant to the Superintendent**

❖ **Chaplain**

❖ **Bailiff (served as accountants, in charge of land and building)**

❖ **Engineer**

❖ **Head gardener and grounds men**

❖ **Lodge keeper and porters**

❖ **Artisans running workshops**

❖ **Head attendants in charge of wards**

❖ **Attendants known as 'madhouse keepers'**

❖ **Cooks**

❖ **Maintenance men**

❖ **Farm staff**

❖ **Butchers**

❖ **Laundresses**

❖ **Tailors**

❖ **Seamstresses.**

Attendants

Male and female attendants could not mix while they were on duty. In the early days, they even entered the hospital through different gates. Segregated by sex just like their patients, many lived in the building and worked at the asylum hospital all of their lives, often for generations. The hospital eventually constructed staff houses on its grounds. They had to ask permission of the Medical Superintendent to marry and women who eloped had to leave their posts. Permission from head attendants was required to go outside the gates for those staff who lived on site.

At Shelton, males were under the head male attendant, and the matron supervised female staff. They didn't receive any medical training, except for some instruction on what was known of mental conditions at the time. They received guidance on how to deal with patients, and they worked across the different wards. Attendants worked in twos during the daytime, always looking out for potential incidents and any acts of self-harm or aggression. They worked at a ratio of one to every thirty patients, although at night, this could be over one hundred patients to one attendant. Attendants also took patients outside into the airing court, which had high walls to prevent them from escaping. Staff sent out non-working male patients to the airing courts from 10.30 a.m. to 12.30 p.m. daily.

There were strict orders to follow from the superintendent and attendants lived in constant fear of inspection from Medical Officers. Checks on them day or night were possible. Spot inspections by commissioners in 'Lunacy' also occurred at any time without notice. Commissioners held powers to discharge patients after two visits, seven days apart. Shifts were long, with daytime duties beginning at 6 a.m. and continuing until late evening when the attendants put the patients to bed. The authority instructed the staff to go to bed themselves at 10 p.m. Some night attendants had a sleep-in role in adjoining areas, with a candle burning all night or one close at hand.

Supervisors expected the attendants to maintain a clean appearance and to act in a quiet, respectful, and attentive manner. The uniform for male staff was a suit without ties, collars or pockets, to prevent a patient from grabbing hold of such clothing during a struggle. The higher the rank, the more braiding they had on the jacket front. At first, the hospital provided women with a long white apron, although they expected them to wear their own long black dress underneath.

Attendants had to be with their patients constantly when on duty. Their role was to calm and occupy patients as much as possible. Supervision during mealtimes, leisure time and during work activities was the norm. Mental recovery involved keeping the patients active and their minds busy. It was both a physically and mentally demanding job and it called for close and continuous observation. It was forbidden to strike or ill-treat patients, although reports of this happening in institutions all over Western civilization were widespread at times of overcrowding and poor staffing.

Female attendants' jobs had two parts, that of a nurse caring for patients and a domestic, cleaning the asylum to keep it neat and tidy. The males had ward duties as well as supervising outside work on the farm and in the grounds. With

supervision, monitoring, domestic duties and physical or artisanal labour, the attendant's day was busy. With board, lodging and food included, a female attendant in 1859 could earn around £17 p.a. working in an asylum, compared to £10 p.a. as a female servant in a private house. However, an attendant was considered a lowly, undesirable job early on, and many young women would choose to work in a town house in preference for the asylum. The reason many generations worked at Shelton was often because their family persuaded them from their own experience that working in the asylum was as a good option.

Training

Until the turn of the twentieth century, the term "attendants" was commonly used to describe nurses. In 1882, Shelton's annual report mentions nurses' night classes were 'well attended.' The lectures were mostly on elementary anatomy, physiology, and immediate treatment of injuries and accidents. Early mental health nurses learned on the job, guided by senior colleagues and long-winded rule books. The Medico Psychological Association of Great Britain and Ireland published 'The Handbook for the Instruction of Attendants on the Insane', famously known as the 'Red Handbook', in 1885. Again, it contains topics such as anatomy and physiology, symptoms of disease, nursing the sick and laying out the dead. Only one chapter is on the actual care of patients with mental illness. The 'Handbook for Attendants on the Insane' was another book published by the same organisation.

In 1905, Shelton started the 'Royal Medico Psychological Association examination' (RMPA). The Certificate of Proficiency in Nursing was until 1921, the only recognised qualification in mental health nursing. It is surprising that the mental health nursing qualification started much earlier than the general nursing examinations.

In 1950, nurse training comprised a Registered Mental Nurse certificate (RMN), and Shelton received approval as a training school.

In 1983, the School of Health/ Nursing built and based near the Copthorne North Hospital (Royal Shrewsbury Hospital) and taught as a diploma.

In 2009, nursing became an all-degree profession run locally by Staffordshire University.

The End of Segregation

When Shelton first opened, people believed it was unsafe for women to come into contact with male 'lunatics. Female staff completed household duties like changing beds and cleaning wards when male patients were outside in the airing courts. Early on, females were making waves for reform, like Mrs Jameson in 1854. She expressed, "the need of good feminine influence of insane men as well as insane women."

The end of segregation started in 1905 with the building of an isolation unit for infectious diseases named Hawthorn Ward.

Required because of the outbreak of tuberculosis (TB), which claimed the lives of 167 people between1905-1910. There had been an influenza epidemic in 1902, where 33 people died and 15 more the following year. The building was situated opposite Shelton's Laundry and remained standing until 1978. This marked the start of female attendants nursing male patients and both male and female staff and patients on mixed wards for the first time.

Not surprisingly, there were a lot of different opinions about having female staff on male wards. Whilst the unions were against it, psychiatrists wanted it, in order to bring asylums more in-line with general hospitals. They felt this raised the professionalism of psychiatry. Some male attendants objected to female nurses being in charge of the ward. Others pointed out that women lacked the physical power to separate two fighting males. This did not consider other non-physical means of stopping a fight. Men also expressed worries that women "might exercise an erotic influence on male patients," who would pose a threat to them. The impact of female staff was more of a soothing, caring influence that calmed patients. Initially, they trialled attendant's wives and noted that the ward became quieter and more orderly, behaviour improved, and the patient's nature 'softened.'

The main hospital remained predominantly segregated until the Second World War, which subsequently led to a shortage of male staff. It quickly became common practice for female staff to nurse male patients out of necessity. Female attendants were even called out of retirement to help (this also happened with retired nurses during the Covid outbreak 2000-2021). Women, who were expected to leave their posts when marrying and starting their own families, also rejoined as paid help.

It wasn't until the 1960s that male staff worked on female wards and in the 1980s/90s, when there were mixed psychiatric wards with both male and female patients and staff. Retired nurse Seevan said he was the first male to take charge of one of Shelton's female acute admission wards (Larch), around 1975.

Pay differences between men and women doing the same job was an issue until the late nineteenth century. There is still a pay gap in the NHS because of gender roles. Many women still spend a decade or more working part-time caring for children or, later, elderly relatives. A lot of female staff still choose family over the demands of promotion, which reduces their wages and pension considerably. However, the whole industry is predominately female now and there are many senior female nurses, managers and doctors.

Previously, staff worked until too ill or frail to do so, although there is evidence the asylum provided some form of pension for the service of loyal staff. The State Pension did not come into place until 1909 and at that time was for the over 70s only. They later reduced the eligibility to women aged 60 and men 65. Ironically, at the time of writing, in 2024, it may go up again to age 71. On a salaries and wages report from Shelton in 1912, the staff were classified as first, second, and third-class attendants. Above them were chief attendants for day and night and head and assistant head attendants for both male and female sides. All paid different amounts that varied greatly.

Staff classification is not that different from the hierarchical 'banding' system now, in terms of rank or the nursing 'grades' of previous years. The difference is that today staff are better supported to advance to higher pay scales with further training and experience. It is just the use of the 'class' system that is disconcerting to us now, as it is so outdated.

If the mid to late nineteenth-century staff received a set of written instructions, they would have read:

Attendants Role

- ❖ 6 a.m. wash and comb patients. Dress them from their weekly bundle of clothes that they use as a pillow which is changed once a week (from 1885 male patients had a second shirt to wear each week once steam laundry was in use).

- ❖ Later: Select clothes that roughly fit for patients from the communal rail.

- ❖ Report any patient illness to the head attendant.

- ❖ 8 a.m. serve breakfast, clean the sleeping rooms, remove any foul straw or linen and sweep floors (It was 1965 before domestics started and only 4 initially, compared to over 40 in the last decade before closure).

- ❖ Attend to patients, observing them closely.

❖ Supervise exercise in the airing court.

❖ Wash day rooms, dormitories, cells and passages, twice a week in the summer and once a week in winter.

❖ All areas to be swept every morning.

❖ Scrub floors made of pitch pine with carbolic soap on the first Monday of the month to reduce dysentery.

❖ Pour slaked lime in the Airing Court privies once a week, empty every 3 months.

❖ Provide pack lunches to outdoor working patients, who are given a "jockey" - a round of asylum bread with an extra half slice on top.

❖ Attendants to organise and supervise patients with ward work, farm and garden work, workshops and laundry work.

❖ Take patients to the main hall where meals are served (later served on the ward as patient numbers rose from 1920s onwards).

❖ Scrape and lime wash or colour walls at least twice a year.

❖ Put patients to bed by 9 p.m. and ensure you are in bed by 10 p.m. to be refreshed for the next day.

Oxon Hall

Around 1930, Shelton Hospital purchased Oxon Hall as an annexe, where they cared for long-stay patients. It is across the road from Shelton, down a track close to the Shropshire and Mid Wales Hospice. The eighteenth-century house, painted white, had a grand regency appearance. Staff slept at Oxon Hall in the 1930s, as it was quieter than Shelton. Former nurse Doris Williams said a man named Sam Edwards transported staff back and forth by pony and cart. Prior to that, the staff slept in a shared room on the wards and were expected to assist during the night if necessary.

Retired Occupational Therapist Helen reported that her aunt Anne Smith was the deputy matron there in the early 1960s and she remembers staying there with her for a weekend at her flat at Oxon Hall. She found the vast kitchen and grandness of the place very impressive. She recalls the patients were elderly females, institutionalised and who stayed for a long time. Retired nurse Tina worked there in the late 1980s with long-stay patients and described a great nursing team. They used Oxon Hall for nearly 50 years before selling and converting it into apartments.

The Grounds

Asylums were deliberately located in secluded countryside areas, and Shelton Hospital was no different. They transported patients there for peace and quiet, but their other intention was to keep them as far away from the public as possible.

The hospital grounds surrounded the impressive main house, reached via a short walk or drive from the grand lodge. Lodge keepers guarded the entrance, watching out for any patients attempting to escape or unwanted visitors. Unlike 'Bedlam' (Bethlem Royal Hospital) in London, the earliest English asylum, the lodge keepers prohibited sightseers. At Bethlem, the curious public once paid two-pence apiece to view distressed patients, like zoo exhibits. People considered it an entertaining afternoon out. Advertised like a top Georgian London tourist attraction, it flagrantly admitted that patients were "often treated like animals," housed in filthy asylums that were "little more than zoos." (BBC History Magazine April 2020)

Visiting Shelton, even for relatives initially, was very strict and regimented. Opening the gate for new admissions and visitors, the first sight that greeted them beyond the high walls were the many trees. They lined the hospital perimeter, and many grew in the gardens. They would be unaware that someone had removed all the Yew trees in 1875 following the death of a patient poisoned from eating the leaves. Other patients copied, which led to the ban by the visiting committee. An orchard around the back included apple, pear and plum trees, used as kitchen produce for fruit pies.

Those entering would notice the serene, landscaped grounds, with gardens, shrubberies, flower borders and walkways. Patients worked on the gardens and allotments as part of their treatment. It provided a welcoming, attractive entrance and the 'country house' had a reception under a clock tower with a pretty oriel window. The hospital had 11 acres of gardens and pleasure grounds. A raised terrace around the kitchen garden allowed females to walk and 'take air.'

In 1856, the asylum developed a farm after purchasing 14 more acres of land. With 300 pigs fed on the refuse ('pig bins') from the asylum's leftovers, there were always pork dinners for patients. They also bought sheep, Ayrshire cattle, and five milking cows. 'Parole patients,' the name for those close to discharge, worked on the farm and even on neighbouring farms at busy times. They received extra bread, beer and tobacco, and some went on the annual week holiday to the Welsh coast. This only stopped in the 1980s. Working on the farm and garden appeared to tire patients out and helped distract them from irrational thoughts, and made them less disruptive. A fire on the farm in 1965 caused £3000 damage and a Foot and Mouth epidemic hit in 1967, leading to a tremendous loss. The hospital sold the farm in 1975 after 119 years.

In 1891, the staff and patients engaged in playing tennis and croquet, and they also built a newly erected bowling green. Weekly dances took place on the front lawn, weather permitting with strawberries and fruit as a treat. Since the site's re-development, Shropshire Homes has moved the bowling green back in front of the old superintendent and doctor's house, Plas Meddyg, its original location.

During the 1960s, patients and staff cared for the feral cats infesting the grounds, despite considering them to be a source of ringworm. Squirrels were always present around the woodland area, and due to the abundance of redwood trees, Shelton was regarded as the last stronghold in Shropshire for red squirrels. When I went back to explore the hospital 2 years after it had been empty, one of the security guards, Shaun, showed me a photo he had taken of a fox and cub playing on the grounds.

They built the chapel within the grounds, and as I mentioned in chapter 1, they expected patients to attend two services on a Sunday in the early days. They only made exceptions if the patients were too disturbed or frail to attend. Memorial services held in the chapel allowed patients unable to attend funerals to pay their last respects. The mortuary was also in the hospital grounds, but Shelton did not have its own cemetery as many asylums did.

Other out buildings provided workshops like the tailor's shop, butchers, maintenance and estates quarters. Eventually it housed a patient's clothes shop 'Unifashions' and a multigym as described earlier on in the book. Eventually, the hospital built occupational, industrial, and recreational therapy departments behind it.

The hospital was famous for its cricket and had a football pitch at the rear. There was a miniature railway in operation at one point. Sport was initially very important to the hospital. In 1927, asylum job advertisements asked what sports and instruments candidates played as so important to them. The calendar of concerts and fixtures for the entertainment of patients and staff was always full. The asylum expected new staff members to join the sports teams and the band if they could play, and to rehearse, practice, and compete in their own time.

Airing courts comprised high walled yards attached to the ward exits, where patients 'took air' and exercised without fear of escape. The hospital administration warned attendants that they would deduct the cost of recapturing any escapees from their wages. The courts separated different 'types' of patients and males and females, of course. A surviving one, long disused, stood at the rear of the male ward Benbow and The Rowans. Another high brick wall attached to Elm was once the wall of a female airing court. They were very basic at first, their only requirement to provide fresh air. There was an outside earth closet privy. In the beginning, male attendants would turn out the patients regardless of the weather, so that female staff could clean the wards.

James Cubin described the airing courts in his book "The Waiting Room to Hell," about his memoirs of working at Shelton Hospital in the 1950s and 60s (sadly out of print and rare to find). He said there was a box full of boots of all different sizes by the exit. The men would grab two, hoping they were a left and right and roughly fitted. Later, the courts contained shelters, drinking fountains, and ornamental features like those found in public parks. Activities like croquet, skittles, quoits, bowls, fives, lawn tennis and badminton became available.

Inside

Shelton's design was a corridor layout comprising narrow, connecting passageways leading to wards on two levels. The long galleries opened into day rooms with dormitories leading from them. Early on, patients slept upstairs on the first floor and day areas were ground floor level. During WW11, elderly wards were all moved downstairs and wards for more able-bodied patients above. This was because of difficulties mobilising infirm patients safely to ground level when air sirens warned. There were no lifts back then. The windows with their small cast-iron frames opened a mere 4 inches (10cm).

They added homely touches, like carpet runners, tablecloths, pot plants, pictures, embroidered and crocheted cushions, and cloths (antimacassars) placed on the tops and arms of chairs. Patients made much of these in sewing rooms on the wards. Bird cages housed canaries and served two purposes; they became frantic at the escape of gas and, when tranquil, provided soothing birdsong. Crockery included cups with a logo saying 'Bicton Heath County Asylum.' After meals, staff carefully collected and counted cutlery to prevent patients from harming themselves or others. In the main hall, able-bodied and less disturbed patients dined until numbers became too high. It remained the centre for entertainment, including Christmas parties, musicals, pantomimes, Tuesday cinema shows and Friday night dances with the hospital band.

Small individual cell-like rooms led off the warren of corridors, to nightingale dormitories, day sitting rooms and dining areas.

Originally, they used some individual single rooms for seclusion or as padded cells. Here, patients slept on straw mattresses in the early days or had no furniture at all if they were a high suicidal risk. The building itself grew with extensions as patient numbers increased. Tall chimney stacks were part of its skyline.

Types of Wards

The gender division originally comprised men to the left and women on the right in equal parts, including the grounds. They then divided each gender into 2 subordinate parts, for the higher and lower classes of patients. They further subdivided these into 4 parts, with the 1st being frantic patients, the 2nd incurables, the 3rd ordinary patients and the 4th Convalescent. As time moved on, there would be no private patients or class systems.

In the last 50 years, wards were based on categories like Acute Admission, Rehabilitation, Continuing Care (long-stay), 'Geriatric' or 'Elderly' Assessment wards, Elderly Mentally Ill wards (EMI), High Intensity rehabilitation (Wroxeter), Pre-Senile Dementia ward (The Rowans) Mental Health and Learning Disability ward (Haughmond) and Substance Misuse Unit (Newhouse).

Ward Names

In 1967, Nursing Officer Arthur Morris renamed the wards that had been numbered for the first 120 years. He named the male wards after famous male Salopians (Shropshire folk) and the female wards after trees! Male wards included Darwin, Sydney, Clive, Benbow, Housman, Hill and Rodney. Female wards were Ash, Poplar, Larch, Lime, Oak, Elm, Maple, Willow, Chestnut, Cedar Millington and Beech. Eventually, there were moves to rename wards after places in Shropshire, like Whittington, Stokesay, Wroxeter, Haughmond, Lilleshall and Buildwas.

The Mother and Baby facility was on Larch Ward (one bed) and then Stokesay Ward at The Marches, a new unit built within the grounds. Patients with puerperal psychosis (now postpartum psychosis) and post-natal depression or other mental health difficulties affecting mum and baby, now go to Brockington Ward in Stafford.

New House - The Substance Misuse Unit was in a separate building at the front of the hospital and opened in 1993. It was a 10 bedded detoxification ward, mainly for patents dependent on heroin, methadone and alcohol. Until the completion of building work at New House, it was temporarily located on Ash Ward.

It briefly became Spruce Ward, moving to The Marches and then closed. There are now no inpatient facilities for those affected by drugs and alcohol in Shropshire. I will describe how alcoholics were 'treated' in the mid 1900s in the next chapter.

Wroxeter Ward - In 1999, the authorities transferred Shropshire patients being treated at forensic hospitals like Ashworth and Raeside to a new low secure unit within Shelton Hospital on Wroxeter Ward. Prior to that, Shropshire paid a considerable amount to other authorities for the care of patients. They transformed an existing ward into a more secure unit, surrounded it with a tall fence, and designated it as Wroxeter Ward. It never qualified as 'forensic,' due to not having a forensic consultant. This meant staff didn't get forensic lead pay enhancement even though most of the patients came from forensic wards. Wroxeter was at the back of Shelton, close to the chapel. It used to be Rodney Ward, a ground floor ward below Housman Ward. When Shelton closed, the low secure ward moved to the new mental health facility, The Redwoods. It became part of the Clee Building, a 32 bedded low secure unit for males with Yew Ward an admission and assessment ward and Willow Ward a rehabilitation ward. Originally, Shelton's admissions reports showed some patients were classed as 'criminal.' But it wasn't until 1864 when Broadmoor 'Criminal Lunatic Asylum' opened that purpose-built high security hospitals took care of the nations "criminally insane."

For 50 years before closure, every day at the same time, they tested the fire alarm. This sounded similar to a WW11 Air-Raid siren, except they used shutters to produce an alternating 'high-low' warning tone. It sounded out a "mournful, melancholy wail that drifted across the fields and rooftops." This quote is a description of the Broadmoor High Security Hospital sirens. This started in 1952 after an escape which involved the murder of a young girl. Sirens at Broadmoor let people know if a potentially dangerous patient had escaped.

The last major escape from Broadmoor was in 1991 when child rapist James Saunders, nicknamed the Wolfman, freed himself. Police deployed helicopters and set up roadblocks. They also informed people in their homes and schools to lock their doors and windows and stay inside. The police recaptured him within two days. Security has improved at Broadmoor Hospital and 12 of the 13 sirens have now gone.

Personal care - Originally, there were one or two earth closets per ward, with one in the airing courts, later replaced by water closets in 1884. But even modern toilets were in rows of cubicles that staff could enter if needed. This prevented injuries and saved many lives, but reduced privacy. Some bathrooms had between 2-3 baths, which were often used at the same time. In comparison, many of the patients' families in these times would have only had an outhouse with a toilet and a tin bath. The water source was a well was in the yard at the rear of the hospital, but this became polluted during storms in 1886. For the next 5 years, they had to cart water from Shrewsbury until they connected the hospital to the mains water supply in 1891. The construction of the Shelton Water Tower took place half a mile away in 1939.

Communication - Telephones were first introduced in 1898. Prior to that, letters were the only way to communicate with the outside world. There was a solitary post box by the main entrance that was often overflowing, and letters reportedly got lost.

Photography - The introduction of photography in the 1880s followed the 'Prevention of Crimes Act 1870.' Taken on admission, they were useful in identifying patients and aided capture if they escaped. Doctors clipped the photo to the case notes and repeated it upon discharge to show improvement. Perhaps the strangest belief at the time was that psychiatrists thought mental illness could be detected in images of patients. Photographs of patients with different mental illnesses were used to aid or demonstrate a diagnosis. In 1856, A Superintendent of a Surrey asylum believed it showed "the well-known sympathy which exists between the diseased brain and the organs and features of the body."

Visiting - In 1892, visiting was strict and regimented, at only once a fortnight between the hours of 10 a.m. and 5 p.m. Many patients had no visitors at all. This led to people quickly becoming dependent on the hospital regime and institutionalised. The deliberate, remote location of Shelton made it less easy and costly for family and friends to visit often. Occasionally, the lodge keeper would turn away a visitor if a patient was in seclusion, suicidal, or if visitors had broken rules. Before telephones, they would not be aware until their arrival.

Reforms - As mentioned briefly in Chapter 7 'The Great Fire,' the 1948 American film "The Snake Pit" drew comparisons to Shelton and other asylums across the country and the Western world. It was based on a true story written by Mary Jane Ward, who had spent time as a patient in a New York Asylum. She hoped the book would show the horrors that a person faced in a mental institution. It showed 'inmates,' considered beyond help, classed as 'incurables,' and thrown together into a large padded cell in straightjackets, which she compared to a "snake pit." Such films, and other media depictions of mental health care, eventually led to reforms at Shelton. These included smaller wards, a renewed heating system, rewiring of the hospital, new lighting installed and redecoration.

The hospital provided patients with shelter, warmth, and a degree of comfort. There was running water, open fires, clean beds, and spacious surroundings. Patients received healthy and varied food three times a day, which included meat from the farm and beverages like beer, cocoa, and tea. However, privacy was minimal with patients eating, sleeping and bathing in crowded communal areas. In the dormitories, beds were so close together during the most crowded times patients had to shuffle to the end of the bed to get out. With very little space for personal possessions, patients kept their weekly clothes wrapped in a bundle and used it as a pillow. They introduced lockers around the 1960s, and working men got to change their clothes mid-week.

Purpose - All the mid 1800s purpose-built county asylums, including Shelton, had a regime based on 'moral treatment.' Pioneered by English Quaker William Tuke (1796) when he founded the York Retreat. He, and the next two generations of his family, offered a new and innovative type of asylum care. Based on what his grandson Samuel termed 'Moral Therapy,' this approach advocated humane and ethical treatment. It contrasted sharply with the existing approach of restraints, beatings, immersing patients in water and bloodletting.

Under 'moral treatment', asylum staff rejected the regular use of straightjackets and the seclusion of patients. With a family atmosphere, the superintendent acted as a 'father figure' to patients. There was a daily structure of chores and recreation time to give patients a sense of contribution. Patients were told that treatment depended upon their conduct. Those who adhered to the regime received rewards and privileges, but poor behaviour resulted in using some restraints or the instilling of fear. The belief was that by treating patients with compassion and kindness and giving them a sense of purpose and normality it would lead to better rates of recovery. It was a way of controlling 'incurable' patients.

Unfortunately, this humane approach to asylum care fell into decline by the 20th century because of overcrowding. As more asylums emerged, the number of people certified as 'insane' soared. With more patients than ever entering asylums, fewer ever left. In 1806, the average asylum housed 115 patients and yet by 1900, the average was over 1,000. Shelton's patient population grew from 104 in 1845 to 1,027 in 1947. 30 years later, numbers had halved and decreased further to only 200 in its final year.

Before 1930, the Lunacy Act required that all admitted patients be certified (what we now call detained or sectioned). Those not 'certifiable' had to wait until their condition became worse. This was due to there being no voluntary patients until this time.

Society segregated inmates rather than providing them with treatment or a cure. Restraint was a means of controlling and managing patients in the institutions, particularly as numbers increased. Many early forms of treatments, which are now viewed as barbaric, were experimental and did not lead to 'cures.'

Regime

Despite attempts to use Tuke's model based on the care of patients in his 30 bedded country house, a replica of such treatment was not as easy or workable in large county asylums. People considered asylums as 'palaces for the mad' in contrast to repressive prisons and workhouses known for their punitive regimes. But their outside appearance was, at times, a stark contrast to the inside. Staff with varying disposition and levels of competence strictly enforced and managed the early regime in an authoritarian manner. Initially, patients had very little say in how they spent their time and none in who with.

Admissions

All asylums were required to have a resident qualified physician, but although reforms were still taking place, the admission of people to asylums was still of concern. After labelling someone as "insane" or if they became socially or economically problematic, someone would call a doctor to assess the potential patient. There wasn't much difference between a lunatic and a criminal lunatic. The fear was that people were becoming a source of embarrassment to their families and would cause them to be sent to asylums, causing a surge in cases.

During the Victorian era (1837-1901) reasons to be labelled mentally ill were determined by any behaviour, unorthodox ideas or actions, considered outside of the rules that define acceptable social norms rules within society. Although mostly unwritten, any of the above coupled with or a lack of productivity or contribution to society could lead to being certified 'insane.' It became a way to remove people deemed socially undesirable from society. Some doctors believed the asylum provided families with an excuse to punish disrespectable behaviour. Also, that it served a social function to control and rid communities of unwanted, difficult family members.

Being diagnosed with 'insanity' meant that you had no rights to refute the decision as you were deemed not of 'sound mind'. Within asylums, the tolerance for odd behaviour and bizarre thoughts and perceptions was higher compared to the outside. I have added a list of the many reasons for admission, including some very obscure ones at the end of this chapter. Although depression associated with various situations was a common reason for admission, others given are much more archaic. Examples included, 'imaginary female trouble', 'immoral life' (often associated with pregnancy or delivering an illegitimate child), 'menstrual problems', 'the menopause', 'uterine problems', 'female disease' and 'nymphomania'

There was a medical belief that most epileptic patients would benefit from living in an institution adapted to their circumstances. At the time, though, seizures were more difficult to control and, before medication, could be extremely violent, and caused significant injuries.

Despite the good intentions of the 1853 Mental Health Act, it appears there was still plenty of scope for abuse of the system. Unfortunately, many regarded asylums as prisons disguised as hospitals. It was a convenient way to remove the poor and incurable from society and, for those with money, private 'madhouses' were often convenient dumping grounds for unwanted wives. Men could send women there if they thought that they had strong opinions or if they were struggling to cope in a family.

With its subjective nature and potential for abuse, 'hysteria' was a reason for admission. If a woman dared speak out of turn or argue with her father or husband, she could be labelled 'hysterical' and committed to an asylum for treatment. All her rights diminished and any possessions or money became the property of her father or husband to do with as they wanted. Society expected women to be reserved, unassuming, and agreeable to the men in their lives. If women attempted to educate themselves or even expressed a desire to read a book, society could accuse them of 'over action of the mind' or 'book reading' and this could lead to certifying them as insane.

Books I used in my research written about women admitted to asylums included "Maria, or The Wrongs of Woman" by Mary Wollstonecraft in 1798 and "A Blighted Life" by Rosina Bulwer Lytton in 1880. "Ten Days in a Mad -House," by Nellie Bly in 1887, and "The Snake Pit" by Mary Jane Ward 1948 described the conditions in mental institutions that led to rapid changes and reform.

The mysterious parallel existence of asylums has always provoked powerful emotions, as it continues to do to this day. But the only prospect of actual change was their inevitable closure and for patients to be admitted to a smaller, modern unit. Despite improved treatment and successful changes to rehabilitate patients and shorten admissions, people considered Shelton Hospital an outdated institution. The outcome of discharge and returning to families and work eventually became the norm as shorter admissions and community care advanced.

KateMcLanachan

By 1959, the radical new Mental Health Act prompted people to ask questions about the treatment of mental patients and the morality of such custodial-like care. This pricked the nations conscious. We now had to justify why patients needed to be locked in, and it became more common for most wards to be unlocked. It was a final break in the Victorian regime, with rightful changes identified and implemented. Enoch Powell described the old asylums as "shameful relics of the past." He made a pledge to "tear down the old mental institutions by 1961," and replace them with a new modal of care based in general hospitals and the community. He foretold the end of the Mental Hospital long-stay wards. The asylum regime was costly, and he had a bold new plan for mental health provision outside of the asylums. As predicted, none closed or had any intention of closing for many years. The focus was still on new medications that altered brain chemistry.

By the 1960s, changes to modernise Shelton Hospital were on the way. An open-door policy gave patients more freedom to walk around the grounds to attend Occupational and Industrial Therapy. With reduced security around patients' movements, they could come and go more freely, leading to the dismantling of gates and high fences. Deinstitutionalisation began by reducing admissions, shortening stays and revolving door admissions, and releasing patients. They reformed psychiatric care to reduce feelings of dependency and hopelessness, making it easier for patients to adjust to life outside of care. The success of psychiatric drugs made it possible, which could reduce the symptoms of psychotic episodes and the need for patients to be confined. Another significant drive was several social and political movements who fought for patient freedom.

REASONS FOR ADMISSION
1864 TO 1889

INTEMPERANCE & BUSINESS TROUBLE
KICKED IN THE HEAD BY A HORSE
HEREDITARY PREDISPOSITION
ILL TREATMENT BY HUSBAND
IMAGINARY FEMALE TROUBLE
HYSTERIA
IMMORAL LIFE
IMPRISONMENT
JEALOUSY AND RELIGION
LAZINESS
MARRIAGE OF SON
MASTURBATION & SYPHILIS
MASTURBATION FOR 30 YEARS
MEDICINE TO PREVENT CONCEPTION
MENSTRUAL DERANGED
MENTAL EXCITEMENT
NOVEL READING
NYMPHOMANIA
OPIUM HABIT
OVER ACTION OF THE MIND
OVER STUDY OF RELIGION
OVER TAXING MENTAL POWERS
PARENTS WERE COUSINS
PERIODICAL FITS.
TOBACCO & MASTURBATION
POLITICAL EXCITEMENT
POLITICS
RELIGIOUS ENTHUSIASM
FEVER AND LOSS OF LAW SUIT
FITS AND DESERTION OF HUSBAND
ASTHMA
BAD COMPANY
BAD HABITS & POLITICAL EXCITEMENT
BAD WHISKEY
BLOODY FLUX
BRAIN FEVER
BUSINESS NERVES
CARBONIC ACID GAS
CONGESTION OF BRAIN
DEATH OF SONS IN WAR
DECOYED INTO THE ARMY
DERANGED MASTURBATION
DESERTION BY HUSBAND

DISSOLUTE HABITS
DOMESTIC AFFLICTION
DOMESTIC TROUBLE
DROPSY
EGOTISM
EPILEPTIC FITS
EXCESSIVE SEXUAL ABUSE
EXCITEMENT AS OFFICER
EXPOSURE AND HEREDITARY
EXPOSURE AND QUACKERY
EXPOSURE IN ARMY
FEVER AND JEALOUSY
FIGHTING FIRE
SUPPRESSED MASTURBATION
SUPPRESSION OF MENSES
THE WAR
TIME OF LIFE
UTERINE DERANGEMENT
VENEREAL EXCESSES
VICIOUS VICES
WOMEN TROUBLE
SUPERSTITION
SHOOTING OF DAUGHTER
SMALL POX
SNUFF EATING FOR 2 YEARS
SPINAL IRRITATION
GATHERING IN THE HEAD
GREEDINESS
GRIEF
GUNSHOT WOUND
HARD STUDY
RUMOR OF HUSBAND MURDER
SALVATION ARMY
SCARLATINA
SEDUCTION & DISAPPOINTMEN
SELF ABUSE
SEXUAL ABUSE & STIMULANTS
SEXUAL DERANGEMENT
FALSE CONFINEMENT
FEEBLENESS OF INTELLECT
FELL FROM HORSE IN WAR
FEMALE DISEASE
DISSIPATION OF NERVES

new candle

KateMcLanachan

CHAPTER 12

PAST TREATMENTS

"I know we must always watch out for 'quacks,' however, most people do not realise that many of the most dangerous, outrageous therapies are the ones approved by the 'traditional' medicine establishment.'
— Howard Dully, <u>My Lobotomy: A Memoir.</u> —

As an advocate for mental health awareness through my job and writing, I feel we must all do our part to help de-stigmatise mental health. Stigma stems from negative attitudes and beliefs toward people who have a mental health condition. Although it may always continue to exist in some form, initiatives over the years to reduce it have emerged through greater public awareness, education, community care, rehabilitation and integration.

Compared to previous generations, many young people today report feeling much more comfortable and open about discussing their mental health. Improved medication and greater access to psychological therapies have led to greater confidence acceptance and expectation of making a full recovery.

Recognising and implementing the importance of service user involvement and carer's support properly allowed for the employment of people with lived experience in mental health facilities. In mental health in-patient and community care, it has been long acknowledged that listening to patients and involving them in decision making, and planning their own care, has had huge personal benefits. New initiatives like

'Patients Know Best' give instant access and greater control over information held about us, all in one place.

In the recent past, negative stereotypes about people with mental ill health as being 'dangerous,' led to irrational and misguided fears, societal rejection, and avoidance, fueled by false beliefs. This followed a few tragic, isolated incidents, where patients released from mental hospitals either stabbed or killed a stranger. The media coverage strongly influenced public opinion, leading to demands that patients, particularly with 'Schizophrenia,' be 'locked away,' and not released. The fact is that most mental patients are at a higher risk of harm to themselves than hurting others and are more vulnerable to being harmed than harming. Also, the media often report the link of mental ill health with violence or portray people as 'criminal, dangerous and evil.' Unlawful killing committed by people with severe mental illness remains extremely rare.

Past Treatments Included:
- **Bloodletting**: Involved taking blood from the vein, cupping and the use of leeches.
- **Blistering**: Some doctors applied caustic substances to the skin to make it burn and blister.
- **Chemicals**: Given with powerful effects producing 'chemical restraint'
- **Injections**: Morphia, Bromides, Chloral Hydrate, Hyoscine, cannabis, amyl nitrate, digitalis and ergot.
- **Purgatives**: Given for 'Melancholia' (depression) to control the digestive system like the rhubarb favoured mild purgative
- **Opium**: Given to 'excited' patients

- **Hot and cold showers and baths**

- **Moral Therapy**: mid 1800s – described below.

- **Mechanical restraint:** padded restraining garments

- **Electricity**: 'straight' Electroconvulsive Therapy (ECT) without anaesthetic and muscle relaxant. This reportedly happened in most psychiatric hospitals, including Shelton before the 1960s, according to a retired colleague who observed it.

Below are a few treatments or methods of controlling patients. I have described these in more detail, because of special interest, first-hand knowledge or personal experiences that staff have shared with me.

•**Padded cells:** Walls and floors were covered with leather or canvas pouches filled with horsehair. This helped prevent disturbed or suicidal patient from harming themselves.

A quote from a commissioner inspecting Hanwell Asylum in the late 1800s deemed them "to have a very powerful effect in tranquillising and subduing those who are under temporary excitement or paroxysms of violent insanity."

•**Restraints**: Unfortunately, there was early heavy reliance on mechanical restraints employed by staff using leg-irons and manacles. They adopted 'management' techniques developed by Renaissance horse-masters to control stubborn horses. Later, staff used straitjackets, waistcoats, and leather wristlets for prolonged periods. The idea of asylums was supposed to be to keep patients safe, but with overcrowding and understaffing, physical restraint was a means of controlling and managing patients in the institutions.

•**Insulin shock therapy** or insulin coma therapy (ICT) was a form of psychiatric treatment in which doctors repeatedly injected patients with large doses of insulin in order to produce daily comas over several weeks.

•**Hydrotherapy**: This was around at the beginning of the twentieth century as water baths, packs, or sprays. Attendants cooled or heated water quickly to produce different reactions in the body.

• **Cold water therapy** could be extreme. Given in short bursts of about fifteen to twenty minutes, it was used to reduce those in a highly excitable or manic state to calm, obedient patients. Treatments varied by institution and doctor, but techniques included:

❖ Tying the undressed patient to a chair and pouring buckets of cold water over their heads.

❖ Restraining patients in cold shower rooms, or shower-baths, and spraying water into their faces and onto their bodies.

❖ Using chairs to immerse patients into small ponds until they were at the point of unconsciousness before being removed from the water and allowed to recover. They could repeat the process until they achieved the desired outcome.

❖ warm baths heated to 97°F given to suicidal, violent and insomniac patients in a dimly lit room which could last for days. They encouraged patients to relax and get some sleep.

❖ Hot or cold packs between 48°F and 70°F. The staff tightly wrapped patients in packs using sheets dipped in hot or cold water for hours.

❖ Sprays comprised warm or cold showers.

People believed that cold water slowed the blood flow to the brain and reduced excitement and physical and mental activity, so they gave it to individuals with manic-depressive psychoses or signs of excitement.

• **Moral Therapy 1800s**: Mentioned in the previous chapter, this was occupational treatment to provide regular work roles and routines to allow patients to fit in as productive members of society. Humane treatment and good quality care helped to 'cure' patients. This was flawed, though, despite being much more humane and the start of the modern mental asylum. Use of comments by its founder William Tuke in 1796 such as, "if you treat an asylum patient like a child rather than an animal, they had a better chance of recovery." Patients had to conform to the expected purposeful, productive lifestyle to 'restore sanity.'

The staff enforced strict rules using a system of rewards and punishments. The idea was supposed to be to keep patients safe, calm and occupied. However, with the number of admissions increasing and overcrowding a problem, physical restraint again became the dominant means of controlling and managing patients in the institutions.

•**Insulin coma therapy**: Introduced to Shelton in 1941. My retired colleague remembers being involved in this treatment, as they constantly monitored and awakened patients to walk around and eat before injecting them again, which went on for several days.

•**Deep Sleep Therapy (DST)**, which started in the 1920s and known as prolonged sleep treatment or continuous narcosis. It was used to keep patients' unconscious for several days or weeks. It is now a discredited psychiatric treatment, as it led to many deaths. My retired colleague recalls they used it at Shelton Hospital at one point.

•**Aversion Therapy**: Administered between 1935-1974. Staff employed electric shocks or drugs to 'treat' the patient, deterring them from conduct seen as harmful or wrong.

Believed to work by creating an association between a behaviour and a negative experience, such as nausea or a painful sensation. The variations of aversion therapy used at Shelton Hospital included:

•**Aversion Therapy for Alcoholics:** Patients sometimes now take medications like Disulfiram in the community to deter them from drinking, but back in the 70s, doctors administered a low dose of a similar drug to patients as exposure therapy. They went to a ward with a table of spirits, accompanied by the nursing staff. When the patients drank and immediately vomited, it was supposed to deter them from drinking, but the staff encouraged them to have additional shots to put them off completely.

Another story told to me was about Martin Conlan, a Charge Nurse who ran an Aversion Therapy clinic for alcohol dependent patients on Benbow Ward. There was a 'bar,' (a table full of booze) and patients wore a wrist band attached to a lever. Each extra shot of alcohol they had led to an increase in the electricity passed through their band. One patient my colleague treated had a high tolerance to the current passing through, which was unusual. When asked how he coped with the shocks, he told the nurse he was an electrician, therefore used to electric shocks!

Aversion therapy for homosexuals: In the 1950s, society imposed similar practices on gay people, considering only heterosexuals as 'normal', and society did not decriminalise homosexuality until 1967 in the UK. The intention to alter sexual orientation was based on the notion that sexual preference was a choice and not innate. Treatments to change homosexuals into heterosexuals peaked in the 1960s and early 1970s. People viewed same-sex attraction as a mental illness.

Although there were always religious objections, it was Henry V111 who first classified sodomy as an illegal act. Many people chose treatment in preference to imprisonment. Only men, not women, faced criminalisation for same-sex relations, but women also received aversion therapy to "cure" them and alter their sexual orientation. Although being gay is obviously not a mental illness, the rejection and condemnation received by gay people did at times lead to depression and suicidal thoughts and actions.

'Treatment' involved giving electric shocks by attaching electrodes to the wrist or lower leg. Shocks were administered as the patient watched photographs of men and women in various stages of undress. The aim was to increase patients' interest in members of the opposite sex by reducing the shocks when viewing these pictures. Another technique was nausea induced using apomorphine as the aversive stimulus. It was less common though, along with another practice of giving oestrogen to reduce libido in males. Whereas we can understand to some degree the use of Aversion Therapy with addictions, this was controversial. Based on antiquated laws and religious beliefs at that time, we know now, as gay people knew then, that this would never work. Thankfully, times have changed and although discrimination and laws against homosexuality still exist in some countries, understanding has come a long way since then.

• **Aversion therapy for Gamblers**: Treatment aimed to reduce the frequency of gambling by using an unpleasant stimulus, such as an electric shock. They aimed this at pathological or compulsive gamblers. As an addiction that can ruin or tear families apart, this was considered just at the time. All participants were willing, and if not, they were persuaded by family and medics.

•**Lobotomy (leucotomy):** This was a neurosurgical treatment for psychiatric disorder or neurological disorder (e.g. epilepsy, depression). It involved making holes in the skull, removing some brain tissue and severing the connections between the frontal lobe and the thalamus. Originally, the doctors drilled holes and injected ethanol into their brains to destroy the nerve connections. They replaced this with an ice pick-like surgical instrument called a leucotome. The purpose of the operation was to reduce the symptoms of mental disorders, but it changed the person's personality and intellect, sometimes making them 'infantile,' or, as described back then, like an 'idiot.' Several long-stay patients at Shelton bore the indentations in their skulls from this treatment performed in their younger years.

Reading that one of the leading doctors who performed Lobotomy's in America, Dr Walter Freeman, was quoted saying, "In some instances, the best thing that can be done for the family is to return the patient to them in an innocuous state, a veritable household pet," is very disturbing.

•**New Drugs -Chlorpromazine** (Largactil): The first antipsychotic drug that came out in 1952. It was initially called a major tranquilliser until the 1960s. It was a significant event in the history of psychiatry. An effective treatment available for the first time that could treat distressing symptoms and decrease the risk of relapse. However, it had very unpleasant side-effects.

•**Other early medication mid 1900s:** Drugs previously used to tranquillise and sedate, included Chloral Hydrate, that was given as a sedative at night. Paraldehyde was another hypnotic drug that needed a glass syringe as it would melt plastic and 'smarted your eyes' drawing it up. A retired nurse said that patients' breath had a liquorish smell when they drank it, but nurses mostly administered it through injections. I remember two antipsychotic drugs well: Thioridazine and Haloperidol, the latter of which is still in use. Haloperidol had side-effects like Tardive dyskinesia (involuntary, repetitive body movements) and akathisia (inner restlessness and inability to stay still) which I remember seeing with long-stay patients at Shelton with schizophrenia.

•**Electroconvulsive Therapy (ECT)**: In the first half of the 1900s, 'mental hospitals' became testing grounds for controversial treatments such as electroconvulsive therapy (ECT) and lobotomy (leucotomy). These methods helped some patients function again, but others felt irreparably harmed, particularly after Lobotomy's which could change the patient's personality. Such therapies became widely used because doctors and nurses wanted to offer patients innovative treatment. ECT and lobotomy, however, reinforced an old and persistent image of asylums as intimidating places of last resort. Around the same time as the development of ECT came the discovery of chlorpromazine and both enabled many patients to be treated and go home.

Some people assume ECT stopped years ago. It did not, although its use has declined dramatically over the years. It remains a lifesaving treatment for some patients with intractable depression. Unlike when it first came out, when patients only had a lumber puncture, patients are now given a short-acting general anaesthetic and a muscle relaxant.

Doctors intentionally pass electricity through your brain, inducing a small, brief seizure which relieves symptoms of major depression. Side-effects are temporary, like short-term memory and confusion, and quickly pass. A course of ECT treatments can provide significant relief from severe depression. Although there is still some controversy surrounding it, the myths of brain damage appear to be associated with the term 'electroconvulsive,' but there is apparently little evidence of this. Given the misery and anguish of depression and the risk of suicide, starvation and debilitation, it still has a place in treatments available, as a last resort, when all else fails or there is no time to wait.

A retired colleague remembers hearing of two senior doctors administering ECT. He said they were both allegedly prone to depression and there was the rumour of an agreement that when it occurred; they administer ECT to each other.

• **Behaviour Modification** (Token Economy): When I was a student nurse on Beech Ward, a rehabilitation ward in the 1980s and 90s, Token Economy, a behaviour modification programme, was in place. This rewarded patients who completed daily living tasks or exhibited behaviours agreed with staff. Patients could exchange the tokens awarded for privileges or desired items like cigarettes, snacks, recreational materials, and hygiene products.

•**Trauma in Veterans**: During the war years, the war office commandeered Birmingham and Talgarth Asylums for wounded soldiers. This led to an influx of mental health patients to Shelton from these two hospitals. Hospital care became custodial care rather than rehabilitative.

Soldiers returning psychologically damaged from fighting in the war did not always receive the help needed. Many considered Shell Shock not masculine, so it failed to get properly addressed or spoken about it. Even after recognition following the First World War. People sometimes considered soldiers with mental health symptoms as cowards, malingering, or faking symptoms to get out of fighting.

Only 28 Shropshire service veterans were admitted to Shelton, a fraction of those thought to have been deeply affected. It is a sad reflection on society's image of war hero's as being strong and unscathed, and with their invisible wounds discounted.

In Word War 11, they reclassified the psychological effects as battle fatigue, exhaustion, and combat stress. But Veterans' symptoms often got wrongly diagnosed as depression, schizophrenia, and later personality disorder rather than a distinct trauma diagnosis. In 1982, following The Falklands War, researchers confirmed a connection between 'hysteria' and the trauma of warfare. PTSD (Post Traumatic Stress Disorder) was recognised only after the Gulf War of 1990/1 and treated using specialised trauma therapy.

Occupational Therapy (OT).
Started in 1932 by Miss Yaxley, who initially occupied a small room on the female Willow Ward. OT introduced handicrafts like needlework, crochet, sewing, knitting and making and repairing material items. In 1947, they introduced it on the male wards and originally called it 'diversional therapy.' In May 1997, they built The Marches, which comprised 2 new wards, the hospital pharmacy, a new ECT Suite, physiotherapy, and a recreation room, and they attached it to the OT department.

The term 'basket weavers,' came from when early Occupational Therapists taught shell-shocked soldiers, often blinded, to weave baskets. It was part of their rehabilitation, plus a distraction, and helped towards the war effort.

Helen, a retired Occupational Therapist remembers her aunt Anne Ward (nee Smith) as one of Shelton's' first OTs. Before that, she was deputy matron at Oxon Hall. She then completed a course in social work, her 1965 essay was on the setting up of a psychiatric hostel for partly recovered mentally ill persons needing rehabilitation in Shropshire. This allowed patients who needed supported accommodation but not hospital admission, to live more independently in the community. Helen herself followed in her aunt's footsteps and she also remembers teaching women to budget, shop and cook meals in preparation for greater independence upon discharge.

Industrial Therapy (IT).

Whilst needlework, crochet and other more 'female' pursuits in place at Shelton since the beginning, not all male patients were physically or mentally fit enough to do the more 'masculine' activities of farm or gardening work. Neither did some have the ability or concentration to do more skilled trades provided, like tailoring. In 1966, Shelton introduced what would become known as 'industrial therapy,' on Benbow Ward. It offered repetitive tasks that patients could easily complete. More importantly, it served the purpose of helping distract and occupy patients. It often involved dismantling or putting something together, hence changing it into a useful commodity. Doing this whilst in the company of others meant they also received stimulation, encouragement, and praise. Often, patients experienced an immediate and positive change in their communication skills and ability to interact amicably with others.

In 1966, the hospital opened a purpose-built unit within its grounds. It had a factory type atmosphere with supervisors and payment for work. In 1996, it moved off site to new premises in Shrewsbury called Abbey Works. Providing employment for 50 patients every day, it also taught how to use public transport and gave many long-stay patients a purpose and structure to their day. Jobs contracted from local firms included iron and light assembly work, printing, packaging and engraving. Both men and women attended when I knew it in the later 1980s.

I very much enjoyed my nurse training placement at OT, IT, and the 'Rec' department in 1990. Seeing the benefits patients got from learning new skills like pottery, woodwork, cookery, or enjoying art and crafts, table tennis or a nature walk was very rewarding. Of course, services offer much more than this now, providing both in-patient and community support in mental health teams.

Physiotherapy
Introduced at Shelton in 1984. Jackie, now retired, was a longstanding Senior Physiotherapist at Shelton. She welcomed the recognition of the link between the body and the mind. Her work alongside the ward team involved assessments to advise, educate and offer either exercises or physical activities to improve patients' physical and mental health. With aerobic and strengthening exercises, patients noticed a reduction in pain, fewer falls and relief from physical problems. Patients and staff had access to the multigym, which was in the old mortuary, before it moved to The Marches Unit. I remember planning to go with a colleague one night at midnight on our "lunch break," but backed out when I heard she was off sick and would have to go alone! Many staff used it though at night. It introduced some patients (and staff) to exercise, improving stamina and physical fitness.

My strongest memory of how successful physiotherapy could be was of a patient who had a reversible alcohol related confusional state. (Wernicke-Korsakoff syndrome). She could not walk as she had numbed, painful, tingling feet and had lost a lot of weight and muscle. She had apparently been continuously drinking for weeks, barely eating, and had lost her ability to stand or mobilise. Initially, she was withdrawing from alcohol and reluctant to take any help offered from members of staff, as unsure of where she was or who we were. It must have been so frightening, but the physiotherapists were so patient and compassionate. Eventually her "peripheral neuropathy" (nerves damaged in extremities; hands and feet) improved, with no permanent nerve damage. The combination of vitamins, food and physical therapy, helped her to recover. The physiotherapists helped our patient strengthen her muscles and balance, improving her circulation to ease pain. It was wonderful to see her stand and take her first steps towards recovery, smiling at her accomplishment.

I could write much more about past treatments bringing us up to the current day, but there are plenty of books and articles available with this information. This chapter describes some of the past medical and nursing interventions at Shelton Hospital under its different names over the ages. It's understandable that we judge some of the treatment in earlier times as barbaric, but the medical establishment of the time approved them and we can only hope lessons have been learned. The changes to today's treatment, which is based much more on psychological techniques, sometimes combined with medication with fewer side-effects is very encouraging. I still believe ECT has a rightful place in treating severely depressed people as a last resort. I have seen the difference it makes and would have it myself if ever needed.

As this is primarily a book on Shelton's 'ghost' stories, might I suggest that maybe some of the barbaric past treatment led to residual spirits lingering. Perhaps despite what many went through, it was the only place they ever considered a home.

Particular thanks go to retired Nurse Phil Williams and Retired Occupational Therapist Helen Ayash Hill for sharing their memoirs for this chapter.

KateMcLanachan

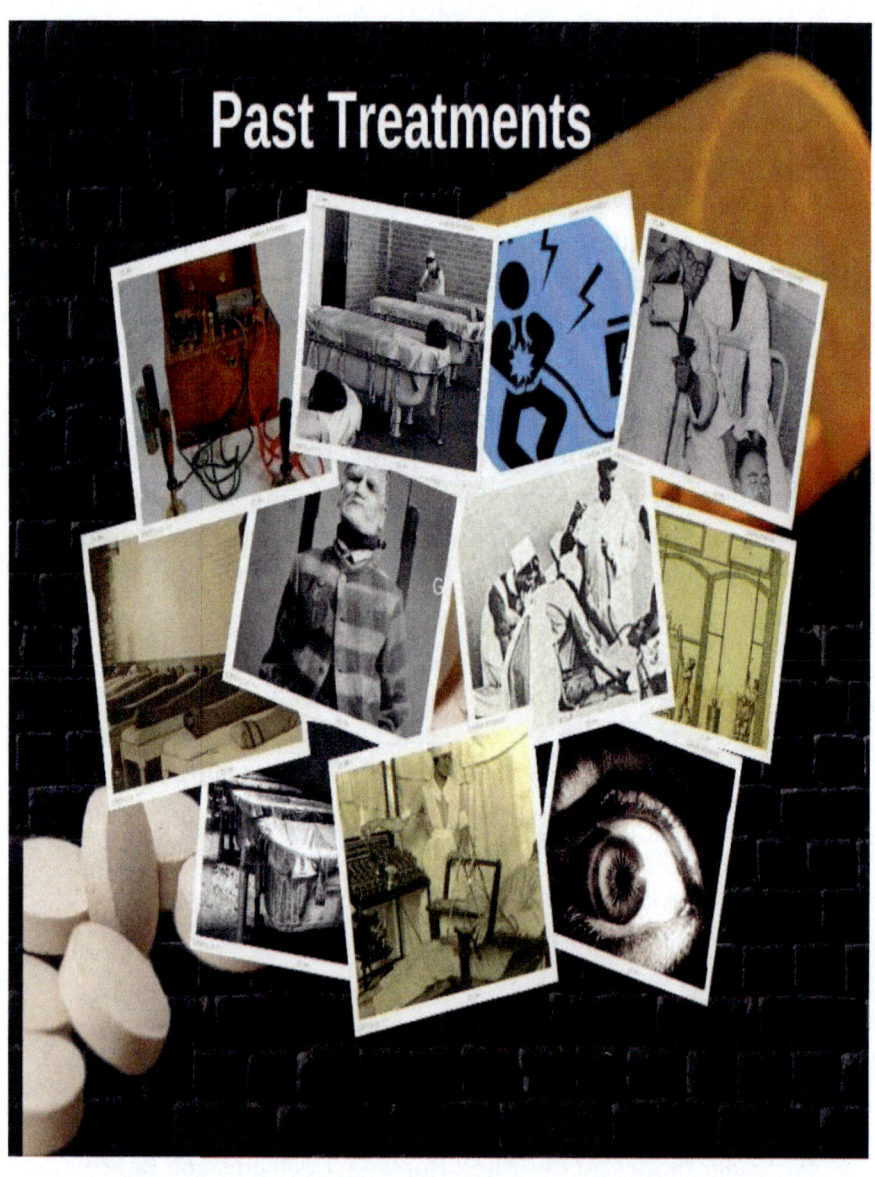

Past Treatments

Ward Names

FEMALE

- A Female 1 (Elm) 1845
- B Female 1 'Up' (Poplar) 1845
- C Female 2 (Maple) 1884
- D Female 2 'Up' (Oak) 1884
- E Female 3 (Lime) 1855
- F Female 3 'Up' (Larch) 1855
- G Laundry (Willow) H 1884
- H Ward (Ash) 1884
- I Female 5 (Chestnut) 1856
- J Female 6 (Beech) 1856

MALE

- A Male 1 (Benbow) 1845
- B Male 1 'Up' (Clive) 1845
- C Male 2 (Hill) 1884
- D Male 2 'Up' (Darwin) 1884
- E Male 3 Refractory Ward (Cedar Millington) 1848
- F Male 5 Male admission (Sidney) 1855
- G Male 5 'Up' (Webb Admission) 1855
- H Male 6 (Housman) 1856
- I Male 7 (Rodney) 1856

Acknowledgements

I would like to say a huge thank you to all the people from our Shelton Hospital Community1845-2012 Facebook page for all their contributions which made this book possible. In sharing their 'ghostly,' unexplained experiences with the group, it quickly generated lively discussions. Memories resurfaced and common themes emerged. I particularly loved reading posts, like when Lorna said to Sandy. "OMG! I can't believe you saw the ball too!" Both had experienced this on Maple Ward, bouncing across the corridor and through walls.

Some sent me private messages and asked to remain anonymous, and others agreed for their stories and names to be shared openly. My contacts at Shropshire Homes, who renovated the hospital by converting it into apartments, swore me to secrecy. But in disturbing the building, they appeared to release more spirits who became active again, manifesting themselves in different ways. Maybe some were angry or vengeful, seeking retribution for the disturbance of their resting place. There appears to be a thin veil between the living and the dead, where the souls of those who have passed on continue to exist. Their residual energy is not bound by physical objects, as they walk through the familiar places they inhabited as it once looked in their former life.

My medium colleagues who visited with us witnessed so many lost souls. Since it was closed, nobody had attempted to cleanse the environment, which horrified Sandra in particular. She felt there was no respect for the past and a disregard for the suffering endured by those who once called the hospital their home. Should we have approached the renovation with more understanding and sensitivity and acknowledged the dark history to bring healing and closure to the spirits that may dwell within? By offering understanding and empathy to those trapped, by accepting their presence and understanding their pain, we may have been able to help those spirits move on to a place of peace and resolution. Or maybe most sightings were just residual hauntings, not ghosts, but a replay of past events. Such 'recordings may play many times, always unfolding in the same way. The spirit is completely unaware and unaffected by our presence and is simply an echo of an event that once passed.

A massive thank you to those who have shared photographs, Lorraine Fletcher in particular, who took some astounding shots of the empty hospital, inside and out. I have attempted to make collages of the photos that link to the subject of the chapters. Lorraine is one of our group administrators and runs "For the Love of Shrewsbury" Facebook group. Cheryl Pearce is our other main admin whose contributions from her long career working at Shelton are remarkable. I wouldn't have been able to make the page what it is without their help and contributions.

I would also like to thank Phil Williams, sincerely, for agreeing to meet up with me at the Loggerheads pub in Shrewsbury last summer (2023). He talked to me about the past treatments he had observed or helped administer. Plus, the many ghost stories he had from his time working at Shelton! It was fascinating to hear about Phil's 37-year nursing career, starting as a 16-year-old cadet so many years ago. Phil worked night shifts for many years, and so has had his fair share of ghostly encounters, too! Along with tales passed down from his dad, Charge Nurse Bob Williams, who worked at Shelton Hospital for decades before him. I learned so much. Thank you, Phil.

Thank you to all the staff who have offered and helped to proofread this book, not only looking at grammar and punctuation, but also whether I have got my facts right! A huge thank you to my friend Andy Taylor in particular, who took the time to go through every paragraph with a fine-tooth comb for me. Also, Simon Bell, a much more acclaimed author than me.

Thank you to my Shropshire Homes contacts for bringing the story alive during renovation. Thank you to the Shropshire Star, for permission to use some photographs of the fire and details from articles published by them over the years. Also, the Shelton Heritage project staff, especially Jessica Kent, for her contacts and information shared.

A huge thank you to Rosie Morris, who worked as a Technical Instructor at Shelton for 23 years and trained as an Occupational Therapist. She is the author of two books about the hospital that were both a wonderful resource for me. "Shelton Past & Present," and "Shelton...eight years on." With so many names changed, I want to say how much I appreciated contributions from our 'anonymous' staff and patients. Thank you, Bonita too, for your wonderful story about the chapel.

Thank you to all the group members, including Kevin, Larry, Bonita, Marie, Tim, Jane, Helen, Karen, Val, Terry, Sandy, Lorna,
Nicola, Simon, Sam, Kevin, Bev, to name but a few. 'Janice and Sandra,' my medium friends and ex-colleagues, were invaluable to this book. I am definitely a believer of spirits after the amazing experience with you both!

Not forgetting a huge thank you to my nursing colleague, Angharad Locke who leant me some books her dad Dave Locke collected. Especially 'Mad Humanity' by L Forbes Winslow 1898 and 'Henderson and Gillespies's Textbook of Psychiatry' by Sir David Henderson and Ivor R.C. Batchelor 1962.

I will use the information that Helen Ayash Hill, a retired Occupational Therapist, and Nurse Angharad Locke provided me more in my next book. Thank you for the long loans; I truly appreciate your kindness.

Lastly, as always, a massive thanks to my friends, family, colleagues, acquaintances, shopkeepers and the local library, including The Writers Lab. Special thanks to Nial and Lyn Evans (torn_paperart) from No.61 in Mardol, Alison from The Enchanted Labyrinth, Ann from Pink Moon Creations and Caroline from Abbey Foregate Card, Gifts and Post Office, Wendy from Connections / Pontesbury PO, and many other bookstores and gift shops who stock my work and have said they will take copies of this new book.

One comment a fellow author said to me on my professional page, which resonated with me, was how unique my position was to write this book. Having trained and nursed at Shelton for 15 years, I then visited regularly as a community nurse until it closed in 2012. My friends, colleagues and contacts also had first-hand experience at Shelton Hospital, so it is not a book based on 'hysteria,' from members of pages on 'abandoned / haunted asylums,' and the like, it has much more to it.

I hope this book will captivate people who have interests or curiosity beyond the 'ghosts.' It is an attempt to offer a glimpse into what the wards, staff, patients and daily life were like. Also, the treatments and history of the building. I have tried to explore alternative views on paranormal encounters, but I can't dismiss the firsthand experiences of myself and others.

Another aim was to get across how much many of us miss the 'old Shelton,' and our work with the patients there. Between us, we have made some unforgettable memories, giving our lifetime's work to helping others and in doing so, getting a lot back. From my perspective, nursing pays the bills, but it is a vocation and requires dedication, hard work and teamwork, but is both rewarding and challenging.

Our cultural views of mental hospitals embed the myth that atrocities were rampant in institutions when open. However, these parts of their terrible history, are not the only legacies left behind. There is a fine balance between the good and bad that took place. And recognition and hope that there were always many staff who felt compassion and truly cared for their patients, despite what we may read in the press and watch on television.

I am currently booked to provide talks about my work to local social groups this year when I semi-retire from nursing (2024). Others have encouraged me to make these facts and stories available on video social media platforms, as it seems to appeal to people outside of the county and those not belonging to a group. I still have the sequel to "The Workhouse Almanac – A Story of Shrewsbury," to finish, which will be another time-leap novel called "Shelton Asylum," based in Shelton Hospital over its lifespan from1845-2012.

My email address is: katemclanachan.author@gmail.com.

I am creating a website.

About the Author

katemclanachan.author@gmail.com

Also, writer of "The Workhouse Almanac – A Story of Shrewsbury." 4.7 *****(45) reviews.

Available on Amazon & in local Shrewsbury book and gift shops, Shropshire Libraries, & Audible & iTunes as an audiobook.

I feel very lucky to be in the unique position to produce my novels and non-fiction books that have both facts and fiction entwined. It works because I write from a historical perspective, using extensive research, passion and fascination in my subjects.

Working as a Mental Health Nurse for 35 years I hope I bring some authenticity to my work, from knowledge and experience. I am still nursing full time at the time of print in an out-patient therapy setting. My books help me look back at life in Shelton Hospital, the former County 'Lunatic' Asylum over the 167 years it was open. This was the hospital I trained and nursed in, as well as visiting patients as a community nurse, until it finally closed its doors in 2012.

K a t e M c L a n a c h a n

Setting up the Shelton Hospital Community 1845-2012

Facebook page a decade ago, we now have 1.3k members. My administration assistants Cheryl Pearce and Lorraine Fletcher, along with the group, have made this book possible and we can now immortalise all their memories and stories in time.

Over the decades, many staff have retired and have relayed their stories through the group and privately, some wishing to remain anonymous. They give many first-hand perspectives on life inside Shelton Hospital.

This book is not just about 'ghosts.' It tells us what life was really like inside for patients and staff, from its early asylum days to that of a psychiatric hospital.

Printed in Great Britain
by Amazon

40194543R00079